Be Yourself, Son

" Always FoRGive youR enemies, Nothing annoys them so much! OSCAR wilde

by

Jenkins R. Fenton

DORRANCE
PUBLISHING CO
EST. 1920
PITTSBURGH, PENNSYLVANIA 15238

Dorrance Publishing Co
585 Alpha Drive
Suite 103
Pittsburgh, PA 15238
Visit our website at *www.dorrancebookstore.com*

ISBN: 978-1-6461-0871-8
eISBN: 978-1-6461-0064-4

I have tried to recreate events, locales and conversations from my memories of them. In order to maintain their anonymity in some instances I have changed the names of individuals and places. I may have changed some identifying characteristics and details such as physical properties, occupations, and places of residence.

INTRODUCTION

From fifteen flights of stairs to a final exam life itself had to give me, the journey had been a tough one. The journey to finding oneself had been a real and a successful one. We are not condemned to fail, and we are not doomed to stay the same person. There is always room for improvement. There is always a way to better oneself. It is just like St Francis de Sales once said: "Do not wish to be anything but what you are, and try to be that perfectly."

One might think once you are in Hell that is it, there is no hope and God has locked the door and thrown away the key. To me, that was not the case, and if God had thrown away the key, I have found it and made my way through Heaven as I was getting better and better and finally got rid of my old ways.

It all started in Boston, Massachusetts, where I was born. I would later be kicked out of my homeland and got introduced to a new one. There is no life without a mother, and that night when I left Boston, I would imply I had died. What I did not know that night was the fact I would be born again. I would be given a new life in a new country, in a whole new world. I would be a new citizen of Haiti. That night I had a new identity: I was Haitian. Three years of age under the brilliant sky of Haiti, I was confused for I did not know where I was at the moment, and the only thing running back and forth in my mind was the fact I needed to see my mother again. I wanted to be in her arms, and I was in desperate need of her love.

Haiti, Perle des Antilles at the time, had introduced herself to me. I was not too fond of her at first, but as time flew by, I have learned how to cope with her. I have fallen in love with her. I was glad I had to see such a beautiful country at that time before its culture started to fade away. That was the place where my ancestors fought for their lives and had chosen to be free instead of being treated like wild beasts. That was the place where the mixing of my blood took place, and this was also the place where my existence had been made possible. Everything was different there, and the holidays were the things that captured my heart the most. Christmas was different. That was the place where you do not need a calendar to remind you it is a holiday. The vibe and the way the day feels will tell you so. Christmas time was my favorite, and that was the time where we used to have little Christmas song contests on TV, and the kids in the neighborhood would put on their best dress and head out at night to throw *pidetwal* and *Pete klorat* around. Christmas songs would be playing everywhere you went, and the grown-ups would sit outside enjoying their liquor, telling jokes, and trying to limit the fun time the kids were having.

New Year's Eve was also one of the best ones. Most people did not sleep, and usually my aunt and my cousin would stay up all night to prepare the *Soup joumou* (squash soup) for the new year. That was the time of the year where you could not go hungry. I have never heard someone say they are hungry on the first day of the year in Haiti. Even if you did not have enough to cook, your neighbors would have your back. That was the time where we used to have each others' back, and this was the time where we knew what it truly meant to be Haitian. Not too long after the New Year, carnival season would make its apparition, and that was the time to forget about any problem you might have had. Just like Christmas, there would be a carnival song contest and live performances at the heart of the city (*Champ De Mars*) where musicians from different groups would perform for three days (*Trois Jours Gras*). Those three days were the ones you did not wish to take away from my fellow Haitians.

Karem (Easter), was one of the holidays I have found to be not too fun. This time of the year, the neighborhood would smell nice. We would all cook some *pwason sale* (salted fish), and that was also the time of the year where red beats were the most used vegetable. On TV, there would be nothing but Christian-related movies, especially the *The Passion of the Christ*. That was the time where everybody would go to church, even nonbelievers (especially in my first neighborhood) and expect to have some nice dinner when they get back home from worshipping God.

As I was growing up in there, I had fallen in love with the country despite the way the government was treating his people. The sun smiled different there, and the waves from the beaches were the loudest. When it rained, it was the best feeling ever. We were allowed to go shower in the rain and sometimes play soccer under the raindrops. Nothing beat that to me. The green mountains, the coconut trees, and the crystal-clear river that flowed day and night while the sound of it helped you fall asleep contributed to the beauty of such a woman. Everything about this country at the time I was a part of it was marvelous, and to me, Haiti was nature itself.

Haiti had become a four-year college to me, but instead of spending four years, I did fourteen. That was where I was sent to learn about life itself, and this is the place you need to go if you want to know the true nature of life. I have witnessed several impossibilities during my days in there as I was on the journey to find and better myself. To me, this was where the word "mother" originated. That was where all the true mothers resided and all the toughest women as well. I witnessed mothers raising their kids by themselves while they were selling candies. Their education depended on those candies and charcoals. There is not much over there, but we Haitians know how to get best out of a worst situation, and for that I admired all of them. I have seen people being successful in a country where failure is king due to the way it is governmentally constructed. My time over there was magical, and it was the best thing I could ever ask anybody.

I was sent there for a reason, not only because of family issues, but because I needed to find my true self. I needed to know the essence of life. *Carrefour, Rue Chez Cator Ti Source* (Hell) was where my dear Aunt Yaya was living when I joined her as a three-year-old kid who could barely speak a word of Haitian Creole. This neighborhood was where everything had started during my second life, and this was where I learned my first life lesson. Yaya raised me in a way nobody else would ever raise their kids. I was raised to be myself; I was raised to experience the good and the evil side of myself. Unfortunately, I started with the evil side, which is why I have named the first neighborhood "Hell." I call it "Hell" not because it was the worst neighborhood, but because I was the most ignorant person living there. It was the best neighborhood, and my worst experiences had happened there.

I would later move to my godfather's house that was on the same street but a few minutes away from Hell. *Carrefour Rue Chez Cator* would be Purgatory. That was the place where I started to figure out how to reason, how to better myself, but I was not better up until I reached Heaven. Purgatory was the place where I have experienced real loss, and that was also the place where my writings had started. It was a beautiful neighborhood but not as lovely as Hell. From Hell to Purgatory, the tests were hard, and I have been preparing for what was to come in Heaven.

Once I made to Heaven, *Paloma, Ruelle Micasa*, I thought I was ready for what I was preparing in the previous neighborhoods, but in reality, I was not. The former communities had been preparing me for Heaven's wrath, and once I entered Heaven, all hell broke loose. Heaven was where I had received a new set of soul. Heaven was the place where

I have become the person I never thought I would be able of becoming. That is my story. It is a story about self-acceptance, growth, and love. That is a story that ends up in a tragic way, which was beneficial. It is that same painful moment that would later bring out the three most important words Yaya had ever said to me. It was not the fact that she loved me. Those three words are the heart of this story. That is my gift to you as I am inviting you to take a look into my second life.

"Every fair from fair sometime declines"
William Shakespeare

CHAPTER ONE

A NEW CITY, A NEW BIRTHPLACE

I was born twice. Nobody ever remembers the day they were born; nobody's ever aware of the whole process. The second time I set foot into this world I was aware of it because I was not a newborn, I was three years of age. I do not remember all the details, but one thing I do remember was the fact I had been given a new way of life. I had switched mothers that day. It was 1995 under the beautiful sky of Boston, Massachusetts, I do not remember all the details, but the cry of a three-year-old kid is still stuck in my head from that night. It was a cry for safety, a cry to preserve a bond, a call for love. I cried, nonstop that night as I fell into hands that were pulling me from my first mother. I would not let go of her loving arms; I would not let go of her caring heart, and all I knew was I needed to be with her. At the time, I did not know if she felt the same way I did. Later I was told she was crying a great deal too. Then came the car ride. It must have been a big car because I remembered, as I was crying, there were two other kids—two boys in the car with me—enjoying their popcorn. I don't know who they were, but I think the reason why they were in the car was to console me. They were tossing popcorn in the air and try to catch it with their mouth, and they were also sharing with me. My mother was not in the car because that would cause more drama leaving me at the airport.

Now, the person who oversaw taking me to Miami did not have a great flight. As soon as he carried me into the plane, the crying started again. I do not recall him not enjoying the whole trip, but I'm pretty sure he could not wait to drop me off. After a while, I fell asleep. Then when I woke up, I was in a different city. The same night, I was passed to another guy whose job was to take me to my second home, Haiti. I do not remember how this whole flight went, nor if that new guy was having the time of his life, but one thing was sure when the plane hit the ground: I knew right away I was home. This guy did not carry me; he allowed me to walk. I was glad he let me walk as soon as we entered the airport because touching Haiti's ground for the first time would play a huge role in the future tasks I would have to achieve. For the first time, I was able to see stars and their bizarre formations in the sky. It felt like this new sky was decorated the same way my mother's Christmas tree was. I was walking among giants. I could not keep my head down. I kept looking up, gazing at the stars, trying to read a new nation's face. There were big lights, very bright inside the airport, and there were tons of people waiting outside, looking for their loved ones who were sharing the same plane as me. We stomp outside after they checked us out and it got loud. It was very loud, but the fact people were talking a different language made it even worse. I was listening to gibberish for a long time. Even the guy escorting me was talking to me in Haitian Creole as he was patting my back.

We waited for a long time outside as I fell asleep on that guy's lap. Finally, a lady wearing a beautiful dress came at us accompanied by a relatively short man, furiously apologizing for their tardiness. That was Ms. Pedro. She was a very loving woman with a friendly face and always eager to help people. She was my mother's best friend. They were very close. They were so close Ms. Pedro ended up being my little sister's godmother, and she practically raised her as her own. For some reason, I felt very safe around her. We got into a car, the four of us, including the driver. The guy who brought me to this new country went back inside the airport as he kissed me goodbye and wished me well. Then Ms. Pedro, the short guy, and I proceeded to the car where we drove off to her house.

As we arrived at our destination, I had received plenty of attention. I had never accepted that much attention in my entire life. Not only was Ms. Pedro loving, but her whole family and even her neighbors were loving as well. I received the welcome of a king that night, and I felt like I was right where I needed to be. Everybody wanted to hold and hug me. They were looking at me and saying things I did not understand. There was that one old lady that night who picked me up and sat me down on her lap. She had a very soothing voice as she sang to me up until I fell asleep.

It was a very cozy house, and I loved it. My favorite part of the house was the dining room. It was painted white, and you could smell the delicious meal they were preparing because the dining room was not too far from the kitchen. It was a joyful house. Everybody was welcome, and there were always laughs. I felt at home, I felt at peace, but deep down I still missed my biological mother. Ms. Pedro took excellent care of me for as long as she could. We developed a bond, and I hoped it would not come down to us breaking it like it was broken with my biological mother.

I do not remember for how long I stayed at Ms. Pedro's residence, but it was not long enough. Of course, my biological mother called numerous times, and I was handed the phone so I could talk to her. One day the phone rang, and it was my first mother. I sat there contemplating Ms. Pedro talking on the phone, but she seemed a little bit off after she hung up. The day went by very quick, but I could tell it was not Ms. Pedro's day. As night fell from the sky, a big, kind of scary-looking guy came to the house. He was driving a nice car, and he allowed me to play with the horn. I later discovered I was about to be leaving Ms. Pedro because mother called and instructed her to let me go live with my great-aunt.

That night when I left, it was not Boston all over again. I was not crying that night. I guess I made my peace with the fact I would be moving from houses to houses, so it was not news to me anymore. Ms. Pedro on the other hand was not too happy about it. I could not tell how she felt that night, but that last look she had on her face as she was watching me go was not too pleasant. It was strange how the whole neighborhood joined in with the same facial expression.

Jean was his name, the big scary looking guy. He'd later become my godfather because I needed to be baptized all over again to receive communion at a Catholic church. The church did not believe I was baptized in Boston. The fact I was baptized twice really proves my theory of being born again in Haiti. Jean and I drove for quite some time. As we were driving, I could spot people on the street going on about their business. Some of them were selling stuff. They did not even need a marketplace. They were walking with baskets on their head and offering people their merchandise. It was a remarkable night, and for the first time I rode shotgun. Jean was a mean guy, and one bad look from him would set you straight. He talked with authority, and you could not do any wrong in his eyes. That mean-looking guy was like God to me. Whatever Jean said, you listened, and whatever you asked, if you behaved, you should have it. He was a father figure to me, and he played a massive role in my entire life.

The drive from *Delmas 2* to *Carrefour Mariani* was a bit rough. As soon as we left Ms. Pedro's house (*Delmas 2*), we drove through other places, and there were mad bumps. It was mostly bumpy roads, and I enjoyed that ride. Jean was playing a song he savored. I did not understand a thing, but the way Jean was moving behind the wheel explained how good it was. We stopped at someone's house. I thought we were done driving for the night, but that was not the case. He had to make a quick stop to see some lady. This lady was not as friendly as Ms. Pedro. She had a mole on her nose, and she looked as mean as Jean. She leaned on my side of the window, gave me a mean look, then she shouted something in Haitian Creole. I knew she said something funny because Jean was laughing so hard I thought an ogre was dying. I just sat there listening to a conversation I was hoping would end soon. Finally, God heard my prayers, and a young boy came out of the house with a paper plate covered with tin foil. He handed it to the lady then she moved to Jean's side and gave it to him as she kissed him and said something I thought was "safe travels." She proceeded by going back into the house as Jean started the car back up then she shouted something else, and Jean stopped the vehicle. She went back into the house and came back with a milk box and some cookies. The lady handed them to me and said something.

I remembered feeling happy to finally have some American food. She then waved Jean goodbye, and we were both ready to hit the road. At some point during the drive, the car smelled like a nice restaurant, as Jean was eating something from the plate the lady gave him. He took my milk box and opened it for me. He did it so badly I could not even use the straw, but later I discovered he did it like that because he wanted me to dip my cookies in there. He looked at me as a proud dad does his son as I was chewing on the soggy cookies. He stopped the car so I would not be disturbed while enjoying my supper. I remember feeling tired, and I was fighting to keep my eyes open to finish my food. The last thing I remembered was his voice singing an opera-like song as I fell asleep peacefully under Haiti's beautiful sky.

CHAPTER TWO

A PRECIOUS ROCK

It felt like I woke up in another dimension after such a horrific drive. That's how bad of a driver my godfather was. It was sunny, and I was lying in a bed that was located next to the wall that separates the balcony and the living room. It was not a bed for kids. It was huge, and I remembered rolling from one end of it to the other. It was a beautiful morning, and I had seen the happiest sun ever. I could spot that big oak tree (*Pye Mapou*) that was facing the house, and I could hear roosters crowing for the first time. As I lay down on those white sheets, I could see the ceiling, painted white with what I was told was a maroon design in the middle. I got up and jumped off the bed, and suddenly I realized I was in a two-story house. On the balcony there were those decorative bricks. They were placed five inches apart, and it gave the house a unique look. As I jumped off the bed, I stuck my head in between those bricks and started examining the whole neighborhood. It was terrific; we had everything we needed. I saw that big oak tree again and not far from it was a river, a small one. That river was so small you could not even swim in it. There were two stores right in front of the house, and the distance between the two stores was a small alley that led directly to the river. They were not big stores we have here in America; they were what we call *boutik*. They were owned by two sisters, and they sold mostly food and drinks. I could see people, primarily kids, taking their morning showers in the river. It looked like they were having fun, and I remember feeling the urge to join them. I could spot people staring at me and shouting words like I understood what they meant. Cars were driving around. The whole neighborhood looked like a Tintoretto painting, given the fact it was so detailed and so colorful.

I pulled my head back, walked past the bed, and entered the living room as I tried to get a sense of the house. This house was impressive, and it was more beautiful than Ms. Pedro's. I stayed in the living room for a while, took a good look at the teddy bears lying there on the big, red couch and listened to the sweet sound of the ticking clock. I remember the sweet smell of coffee coming from downstairs. I tried to follow the scent as I walked past the upstairs bathroom, my cousin's room, and then ended up in another balcony, except this one did not have a ceiling. It was not covered at all. As I was on the balcony, I could sense how hot it was, and it felt great. I kept on following the smell, for I was hungry. I ended up on the top of a flight of stairs that was connected to that balcony that consisted of fifteen steps. As I stood on the first step, I saw an old lady— a lovely lady with perfect gray hair, not too long, and she had a smile that could lift your spirit in seconds. She was wearing a long dress, not a very fancy dress. We called them "*Moumou*," mostly old people wear them in Haiti. She was wearing a blue *Moumou* with artisanal drawings on it, and she had those big glasses she wore all the time. It was like she was waiting for me down there the whole time. She told me to come downstairs by making the "come here" gesture with her hand, and I just did. No one could resist such an angelic face.

She stood down there with open arms, and I immediately put my trust in her as I ran down the stairs and jumped straight into her lovely limbs. She looked happy, and I was pretty sure I was sharing the same feeling as well. We went from the front door, proceeded to the gallery, then ended up into the downstairs living room. The house was very spacious and well-furnished. She left me there on the table while she got my breakfast. I remembered having coffee and a peanut butter sandwich. She took the crusts off the bread and prepared the coffee with all the care in the world. My coffee was different from hers and my big cousin's. They had the grown-up coffee. I, on the other hand, had the same one, but it was mixed with powdered milk. It was delightful.

That lovely lady took good care of me. She did not let me feed myself. She always put food in my mouth as if I was born yesterday, and I liked that. She kept putting food in my mouth up until I was twelve years old. Otherwise, I would not eat. I was a spoiled child. She was everything you could ask for; she was my God, the only person I could turn to when things went wrong. She was my second mother. Everybody in the neighborhood seemed to know about her. All the merchants, the kids, police, and even the dogs, they all knew about her. I did not know her name, but I realized there was a pattern. Every morning there would be a woman calling her out. She used to sell bread and always yelling "*Yayoo,*" and my aunt would answer by saying: "*Woo,*" and then go downstairs and get a big bag of bread. Based on that, I thought "*Yayoo*" was her name, but it turned out not to be. That was a nickname the neighbors gave her, and it was short for Andrea. Sometimes the kids would call her "*Yaya*" which was the way I used to call her whenever I needed something. I would be like, "*Yaya,*" then blurt something out in English, then she would go look for my cousin to translate for her.

She went through a great deal of trouble with me. I would later realize how challenging it was for her to take care of a kid who did not understand her language. Upstairs, we had those big, white, porcelain flower vases. There were five of them on the balcony, and two of them were empty. The other three had beautiful flowers in them, and they were planted in soil, real soil. The empty ones would become my toilet because they looked like the toilet bowl I used to use when I was back home, and they were more comfortable for me to use. I did not have to wait for someone to open the bathroom door for me or to pick me up and hold my hand through the whole process. I could hop on them and do what needs to be done. That was Yaya's biggest struggle, and she had to teach me how to ask when I need to use the bathroom. Not that I did not know how to ask for help, but whenever I did, nobody seemed to understand me, so I took care of it on my own. She bought a little blue vase and left it inside the bathroom, and she always left the door open so I could access it. That was the very first lesson she had taught me, how to use that vase.

She was my great-aunt, and to me, she has been my mother the day I entered that new country. She was the root of the family and the oldest one too. She practically raised every single person in the whole family. When her mother and father died, she had to take care of her two younger sisters. She did not have any kids of her own, but her sisters did, and she was the one raising their kids and all their grandchildren as well. I was the last grandkid she took care of, and all my life she kept reminding me I was going to be the last one as if she was telling me she would not take care of my kids in the future. Maybe she was sending me a message, but I was too young or too ignorant to understand it. Perhaps she was telling me by the time I got my kids she would be long gone. That confused me a lot. Still to this day, I am wondering what the real meaning behind that statement was: "You are the last one I am raising."

To me, she was the starting point of the family. It is almost like when God created the earth, then created Adam. In my mind, when it comes to my family, on my mother's side, God created the universe then he created my great-aunt. I did not focus on who came before her. She was the one I concentrated on the most. Yayoo used to tell me stories about her parents. Her mother used to sell stuff while her father used to be the town's drunk. I could say she did not like her father that much or they did not have a real father-daughter relationship. He did provide for his family, which was good, but I found him to be a hilarious guy, and sometimes I wished I had met him. A few years after her mother's death, her father has passed. She told me the story behind his death, which was a bit funny to me. He died because he drank too much. When he went to the hospital, the doctor told him to stop drinking, or it would be the cause of his death. He came back home and told Yaya about it, and she did what was best, which was hiding his bottles. He then proceeded by saying: "I am not going to stop drinking. Even the doctor drinks." It was one of those tragi-comic stories, and that one was my favorite.

After her father's death, Yaya had to figure out a way to take care of her two younger sisters. I do not remember how old she was when she got into the broom business. In Haiti, we have two kinds of broom, "*Bale pit*" which is the one we use indoors and "*Bale pay*" which is the one we use outdoors to sweep the leaves and trash that are in front of the house. She knew how to make the indoor ones, and that was how she managed to put food on the table and make sure everyone was happy. She did not mention any other family members helping her. It looked to me she handled things on her own. That was the reason why I believe her to be the first, the head of the family. She was our Eve.

After a few years in the broom business, she would later meet a guy. I do not remember his name, but he was a fisherman. He was a good man, as he took good care of her and her sisters. I would consider him to be Adam. Things were good for a while, but life happened as he died, and Yaya went back to square one. Ever since that man, Yaya swore to be by herself for the rest of her life, no more man, just the three sisters. Cleante, the younger one, ended up being pregnant and gave birth to Jean, the guy who drove me from Delmas to Carrefour. She gave birth to my godfather, and that would cause Ana, the second sister, to get into the "*Fritay*" business. *Fritay* is fried food like plantain, potato, and some meat, especially pork (*Griyo*) with a spicy type of coleslaw we call "*Pik-liz*." Ana knew how to cook. She was pretty good, and business was booming. Just like that, they made some good money and ended up moving somewhere else.

Ana was my grandmother. It was because of her I was born in the United States. Her first son, my favorite uncle, managed to travel to the states and then sent for his mother, and together they brought the whole family here as well, except for Yaya. They did not send for her not because they thought she did not deserve it, but because she could not imagine living somewhere else. All her life she had been living in Haiti, and she could not bear leaving it behind. She used to tell me, "Haiti is the most important part of my body; it is my heart." They have tried to convince her, but of course they were not successful. One thing I admired about Yaya was the fact that once she put her mind into something, she would not stop until she completed it. She did not want to go to America, and there was nothing you could do to make her change her mind. She stayed in Haiti and received with an open heart all the grandkids and raised them as her own.

My grandmother, Ana, built this new house. Yaya was practically the owner of that house. She was the one taking care of it and filled it with nothing but love. It was a big house, and I thought Yayoo deserved it. She had to hire a maid to help her take care of it. I was the only man in the house, and that made me a little bit different—different in the sense where I could see the world on both sides and know what it is like to be treated like a woman in Haiti.

Most people only know one side of themselves. They do not even bother to wonder what it is like to feel or to be in someone else's shoes. For example, I was born a man naturally, and that is the only side I am supposed to know. The truth is, you must know how the other gender feels for they are also human. You must at least try to understand them. Just because they are women does not mean they are limited in life. I have lived that, and I have seen the wonders women can accomplish. I grew up being the only man in the house, and that felt good—not because I thought I was the man and everybody else was below me. That felt great because I had the opportunity to know and experience the struggles of being a female in a country like Haiti.

Yaya was a very religious woman. She would not admit it, but I believe religion played a significant role in the family's separation. I am not against religion. I think everyone has the right to choose and follow any religion that meets their needs. I've had my own experience with religion. I was once a Catholic. I was a Catholic not by choice. I did not know how it happened, but it did, and I was glad. My aunt was a protestant and was not in favor of Catholicism, but she allowed me to attend the communion, and before you know it I was a Catholic kid. With Yaya, I always had a choice. She raised me in a way I think nobody in this era would do, especially in Haiti. She brought me up by letting me be me, by allowing me to have the personality of my choice. She allowed me to learn stuff by myself and always told me that option is something that is not rare. I will find it no matter the situation I find myself in. I was also punished or disciplined whenever I did something terrible, but not by her. She did not have the heart to punish me. I was not raised to be a puppet. I was not raised to do everything I was told, no matter what it was. She showed me the way, and it was up to me to choose the right one and make the right decisions.

I grew up watching my aunt go to church every Sunday. After my communion, I stopped following her path, and that caused me to go to a different church. After church, we would sit and talk about what was preached and have a little debate. It was fun for a while up until I decided to stop going to church. Yaya was okay with my decision. I ended up visiting her church, which was no different than mine, and before I knew it I was a member. I was no longer a Catholic. I was a protestant just like my aunt. I kept at it for a while, and another decision was made. I stopped going to church because some stuff did not make any sense to me. Once again, my aunt respected my choice, and we just kept on loving each other.

My grandmother practiced voodoo. That was her religion. She had built a *peristil,* which is a place used for voodoo dances and ceremonies.

She created that place out of respect for Yaya's religion. Ana started to practice her faith in the house. Then she realized Yaya was not too comfortable with it, then she went ahead and built up her temple. That temple was the size of a fortress, and I have participated in some of the voodoo ceremonies that were led by her. She was the voodoo priestess, and my godfather, Jean, was the priest. Yaya never thought voodoo was wrong, but she believed it would not show or lead you to God's kingdom. I believe every Haitian understood practicing voodoo was worshiping the devil. I've never thought of it this way. All my life I've never heard my grandmother or my godfather achieved evil things to people. To me, it's what makes us Haitian; it is our legacy; it is our birthright. That same legacy would later put a distance between two loving sisters. At least, that was what I thought the reason was.

Yaya was the family's life support. Whenever someone was coming to visit from the United States, especially family members, she oversaw taking excellent care of them. Friends became family, and so did strangers. Everybody in the neighborhood was welcomed in our home. Yaya would have church gatherings in the house where every member of her church would come in and have a full day of prayer. We call those gatherings "*Jèn*." I loved those days because not only did I have to help my lovely cousin move the furniture so everybody could move around freely while worshiping God, but I had the privilege to cook with her and eat her tasty foods. It was almost like a party, but it was one for God's worshipers. I did not fully participate in those gatherings. I usually stayed upstairs in the balcony listening to the chants and prayers. I would come downstairs to say hi and kiss everybody in the lobby when they were done. That would be a Haitian habit. If you grew up with a Haitian parent, if they had visitors, you must salute them and kiss them. Those were the best of days, and the atmosphere changed too. After the worshiping, you could tell the house had a different vibe. It became a humble house, and I would sleep soundly that day because my mind was at peace.

I have lived my life, and still am living it based on one line from William Shakespeare's sonnet eighteen that says: "Everything beautiful sometimes will lose its beauty, by misfortune or by nature's planned out course." This line has made me deal with death a lot differently from other people. This line made me see the world differently. That is the way of life; it comes and goes, and maybe comes back around. Yaya ended up passing away, and still to this day, I refuse to accept she has passed. She cannot be dead, not while her legacy lives on. As long as we are breathing, as long as our hearts keep on beating, so does hers. The way I see it is Yaya was a painter, and the rest of the family is her most famous painting. As long as that painting is still here, there is value to it, and its fabricator lives on through it. Just like she used to say: "The greats never die; they live through the hearts inspired by their oeuvre."

She has been and still is an inspiration, and that is something that can never be taken away from anybody. Just like her favorite passage from the Bible states: "And I tell you that you are Peter, and on this rock, I will build my church, and the gates of Hades will not overcome it." (Mat 16:18). I have been her rock, and upon that rock she has built her life's most precious work, and nothing can take that away. I was lucky enough to be the foundation of her work.

CHAPTER THREE

THE CREATOR

Everything has a starting point. Mine was my grandmother, Ana, my great-aunt's sister who went through hell to raise her first child, my Uncle Daddy, according to my Great Aunt Yaya. Ana was the reason why most of the family today is living in the States. She was my hero, and because of her I get to be called an American. According to my great-aunt, her sister Yaya, she was a great cook and an excellent dancer. One day, she decided to get into the food business. She had a house not too far from Yaya's, and that was where her profession started, and that was how she managed to take good care of Uncle Daddy. She created many enemies just by starting this business. There were other women in the area who used to do the same thing, only my grandmother was the best, and she got all their customers. That did not stop her from doing her job; she kept active and fought through the hard times. Friends became enemies, and enemies became the devil's associates. There were death threats and many accusations of Ana being a *lougawou*, basically a witch.

It was hell on earth for my grandmother, but she managed to survive and raised my uncle to be the finest young man in the neighborhood. The business helped pay for his school and put food on the table as well. My uncle's father was not around that much. Let's say the sisters did not have any luck with men. Ana had no idea she gave birth to a savior, the one in my eyes, who would push the reset button for the entire family. I do not know the story entirely when it comes to my Uncle Daddy, but let us just say that Daddy met a young woman, and she happened to be spending the summer in Port-Au-Prince, and from there, magic happened. I just stick to that story because it is the one that make the more sense to me, and to be fair, I love me a love story. They fell in love and kept in touch through letters. They were very intimate letters, and I was bummed out when I realized most of these letters were from my cousin's boyfriend. His lover did manage to get him in the States, and from there, their family grew, and Daddy managed to get my grandmother here as well. After my uncle was born, my grandmother gave birth to four other kids, all women.

Before my grandmother made to the U.S.A, she lost her business a month before Daddy left Haiti. I was told one of the other women doing the same business did some magic, and one day all of my grandmother's meat and produces went bad, maggots everywhere, and her cooking goods all went to flames. It was a tragic moment for her, and she resulted in moving to my great-aunt's house, which was their parents' house. Together they fought through the hard times, helped Yaya with the *Bale* business and took care of their younger sister, Cleante. All three of them stayed in *Bel-Air* (Their hometown) for quite some time until Daddy and grandmother left to create a new path for the entire family.

Now with both my uncle and grandmother in the States, it was time for them to send for the rest of the family in Haiti. Yaya was in charge of her younger sister and my four aunts. Ana was sending money to take care of my aunts, and Daddy was also throwing my great-aunt some money as well. With that money, Yaya managed to leave *Bel-Air* and moved to *Fontamara Carrefour*. She lived a couple of blocks away from my grandfather's house, my mother's father, Felix. She rented a three-bedroom house in which five people resided, and you could only imagine how it got when Uncle Daddy and grandmother came to visit them. It got packed. After a few good years had passed, Daddy and his mother got together and saved up then bought a considerable amount of land in Chez Cator Street, Ti Source in Carrefour, and built my dream house where I grew up. My aunts and my mother did not have the chance to set foot in the house when it was built; they were long gone to the states. Ana had sent for all of them.

Now with Yaya all alone, Daddy had arranged for my cousin Dannie to move in with her in the new house. Dannie was my uncle's daughter. When she was thirteen years old, her mother died in a house fire, and ever since she was living with her mother's family up until my uncle had sent for her so she could stay with my great-aunt in a better neighborhood. Together, they took care of the house, and they were the ones to cook whenever my uncle or my grandmother came to visit. We hired a maid, but she was only there to help with keeping the house neat.

For some reason, my family did not let strangers cook for them. Maybe they did not want to share their favorite recipe, or they might think nobody could prepare food better than them, but we fed ourselves. For the cleaning part, we needed an extra hand because the house was too big. There were two master bedrooms downstairs, a dining room, and a living room. The living room and the dining room were separated by a large hallway, which led to the kitchen on one end. On the other end it led to the garage where I used to keep my toys and the stray dogs. There was a small bathroom (not complete, just a concrete bathtub) and a restroom not too far from it.

On top of the bathtub were the fifteen steps that lead upstairs. As soon as you opened the front door, you could spot the stairs on your right, and in front of you was the downstairs faux balcony. We would call it a "galeri" which is a part of the house where you can receive guests and sit there and have a great view of the neighborhood. The stairs led to the upstairs balcony where my aunt kept her flowers and other plants and big barrels of water to water them. I would later come up there with my friends to plant corns. That balcony was not covered, but we had barbed wire on top of the walls. There was another big hallway that led to another master bedroom straight ahead, my cousin's room on the far right, the guest bathroom next to my cousin's bedroom, and the living room on the left of it. There was another balcony that was connected to the living room, and from there, you could access the master bedroom through a wooden door. That wooden door looked like it was designed in Egypt. It had some strange marking on it, and it looked like it belonged to a palace, not a house.

We would all sleep upstairs in the balcony that was connected to the living room. Both my cousin and Yaya would make their beds on the floor, and I would have the twin size bed to myself. When my uncle and grandmother are visiting, I would make my bed right next to my great-aunt's and let my grandmother use my bed. My uncle would use the master bedroom, and my cousin, his daughter, would make her bed on the floor right next to my grandmother's. Those were the best times where we would all lay down and tell jokes, and we could hear my uncle laugh through the wooden door like an ogre.

I remembered when I met my grandmother for the first time. I was six years old, and I was the most innocent kid in the neighborhood. I knew it was going to be a big day because my cousin and great-aunt went to the market and bought lots of groceries. We had people coming over and helping with cleaning, trimming the trees, and helping with dinner, but they weren't allowed to cook. After a long day of working on the house, it was shining, and it smelled of roses. I remembered Yaya dressing me up and my cousin getting ready to welcome the guests.

I sat on the upstairs balcony that was uncovered, and my eyes could not move past the front door. I was passionately waiting to see my grandmother for the first time. I sat there for about an hour and a half, and there I heard it, a car honking. My great-aunt rushed to the door with tears of joy while chanting about how much she missed them. I sat there with my little heart ready to leave my rib cage and roll down the staircases to meet my grandmother. A few minutes went by, there she was…the woman I long awaited, the woman I had heard so much about was just fifteen steps away from me.

As she was making her way to the downstairs balcony, my presence interrupted her walk. She spotted me sitting up the stairs with my legs crossed and she had that smile like she knew me before and could not wait to see me again.

"*Oh Letenel!* (Oh Lord)," she goes, "*Gade ti Mireille!*"

That was her way of letting people know I was the spitting image of my mother (*Mireille*). She dropped her purse as she was telling Uncle Daddy not to help her up the stairs. She made it to the top of the flight of stairs, and she picked me up and immediately, my hands could not take it anymore. I had to hug her. I remember the sweet smell of Caribbean perfume on her outfit. I could feel her teardrops on my back as she was crying and turning me around. To me, she did not look that old for she was so strong and good looking. She held me there for a good minute then she finally let go of me. My uncle gave me a firm handshake and went on by saying: "He is a man already!"

I ran to my cousin's room as I hid the rest of my body behind the door and pointed my head out to keep tabs on such a beautiful woman.

I witnessed a few men in the neighborhood who helped bring the luggage upstairs as I was still taking my sweet time to contemplate my grandmother. Before I knew it, it was time for supper. My great-aunt usually fed me, but this time I wanted to be like everyone else. That day, I retired from Yaya's lap and her delicate hand landing food in my mouth. For the first time, I had a spot on the "grown-up" table. I remembered not being able to reach the table as I sat on the big chair, but thanks to my genius uncle, he spotted the couch pillows and stacked them up under my butt. That was the comfiest chair ever, and it made supper a whole lot better. I could not keep my eyes off that angelic figure that was sitting across from me—short, curly hair with a smile that came and went as she made eye contact with me, silky smooth-looking skin and eyes that were so alive it would turn one into a humbler human being. That was my first official supper, and for the first time I had a glimpse of my dream, which was to have a big family.

"Come here, and let me bite you," Ana would say to me sometimes when I was feeling down or when I had done something unpleasant.

I do not think there is anybody in the whole world who could love her more than her son did. Daddy would do anything for her, and there would be no life left on earth if she was not a part of humanity. There was no way to break that bond, and together they achieved a lot of great things for this family. As for my grandmother, she loved all her children and grandchildren with all her might.

There was not a day in my life I do not remember feeling her love; even though she was miles away from me, the thought of her always brought joy to my heart. Even in her darkest moment, she would not act as most Haitian parents did. She would not take it out on you. Besides, my grandmother would be calm and let the presence of her descendants rejoice her as she was fighting her demons. I could not have asked for more. She was more than a grandmother. She was a friend when you needed one, and for me she was nothing more than a guardian angel and still is.

Many people would agree with the fact if a mother did not raise her child, if she was not present in the kid's life, then she is classified as a bad mother. What they seem to forget is there are circumstances where these sorts of situations happen. Yaya was everybody's nanny; she was the whole family's mother. She helped raise all of us, and she raised her sister's kids as well. Does that make my grandmother a bad mother? I do not believe so. They only thing that matters is her kids could feel her love from miles away and she provided. She was not there physically, but in all our hearts she remained present. Life will plant all type of obstacles on your way to your destination. Some of them you will surpass, and some of them you will never be able to break even if you've traveled back in time. The most significant and unbreakable obstacle life had thrown at me was the fact my dear grandmother had passed, and I had no chance of showing her how much I loved her. People would reassure me she knew and she was proud of me. All of that did not matter. The fact I did not show her such love had become a chain on my feet, keeping me from moving past her passing. Many people who know me well will tell you I have no heart, they will tell you I cannot feel, but that is not entirely true. As a kid, I used to shed tears for no reason. Now, it seems like I ran out of those tears. The idea behind all of this is plain and simple; it is the last lesson Ana had taught me. She once told me: "When I'm gone, the tears running down your cheeks won't bring me back to you...the only thing that will keep me close to you is your smile, your happiness, and that is the secret on how you are to keep me alive within your heart."

CHAPTER FOUR

STRANGER IN DISGUISE

I called her "The quiet one." Not to Yaya and Ana, she is not. They would describe her as "The reckless one." The time has come for me to introduce you to the third sister, Great-Aunt Cleante. She was a mysterious one, and you could never figure out what she was planning. She was, most of the time, really calm and always humming some old songs. She was the second one to leave Haiti for the United States not too long after Ana left. Like my grandmother, before Cleante left, she already had kids in Haiti. She had three children, and one of them would later become my godfather. Yaya was supposed to be the second one to leave the country, but she kindly refused the offer. She acknowledged she was getting old and she was not ready to adjust to a new environment. Haiti was the only place in which she claimed she felt safe. That was her home. That was the only place that kept her heart going. When they were young, Yaya would focus on Cleante more because she was the younger one, and she was not ready to make decisions on her own. Yaya would tell me on Sundays she would do her sisters' hair after giving them their bath. My grandmother, Ana, would be a good girl and keep herself clean, but Cleante, right after her hair was done, she would lie on the dirt and go under the stove and put ashes on her perfectly braided hair. Yaya had a hard time with this one. She would go around the neighborhood and pick fights with other kids and sometimes, Yaya had no choice but to keep her inside by tying her legs to one of the house's doors.

As she was growing up, she would get wiser and act appropriately. She became more mature than the other two, and before you knew it, she started to be more responsible and more docile. She would give birth to her first son, Jean who was my godfather, the meanest person I have ever met, and he was like a father figure to me. Her first kid would welcome her to reality, and that was her favorite kid. She loved him more than anything else in the world. To her, he was not capable of doing anything wrong. He was the perfect son in the world to her. Not too long after giving birth to Jean, she had her second son, Ernst. Ernst was the coolest one to me; he was very handy. He could fix anything. He made my childhood a little bit productive. He would teach me how to repair bicycles, sinks, and radios. Ernst was the spitting image of Cleante and the least favorite. He was the coolest dad anyone could have.

Ernst would fix people's stuff for a living, and that would explain why his house was so full of electronic parts. One thing he taught me was all the junks had value; you never knew when you were going to need one. Like my grandmother, he would call me *"Ti Mireille."* He would never give me money; he wanted me to earn it by helping him fix broken stuff. That was his way of telling me nothing is free in this world. You'll have to work hard to earn things. Anything you want, you will have to sweat to win them. With this business, he managed to raise four kids and lived a decent lifestyle.

As for Jean, the only thing he ever did for me was give me an ass-whopping whenever I did something wrong or when I was a bad boy. He was know known as what most Haitian women nowadays would call a "True Haitian man". He had many women, and he had a lot of kids. He knew how to seduce women very well and sometimes I wished he had the time to teach me his secrets. He was a big, tall, scary guy, and you could hear his voice from a mile away. Whenever he was coming over, I would hide somewhere until his ogre-like voice would call my name, and I would show up, trembling like a terrifyied, wet dog.

"I am fine," I would answer to him whenever he asked me how I was doing.

I could not say otherwise because the conversation would be too long, and I could not bear standing there and explain every single detail about how bad I am doing. You could not have fun around him; a dark aura surrounded him. Everybody could see that. When he was around, the mood changed and the sky would always turn gray, and sometimes it would rain when he showed up in the house.

Two dogs would keep him company—Beethoven, the brown one, and Maiko, the furry, white one. All three of them would make my day very difficult and very memorable. After questioning me, Jean would give me ten dollars, so I could go and buy some *frites*. I should be happy whenever he gave me some money, but the truth was I took the money, walked away with my head down, went upstairs, and put it in my piggy bank. I never used his money, I saved them up, and I later used them to buy drinks and a nice bottle of champagne for Yaya's sixty-eighth birthday.

Cleante's third kid would be Gladys, a daughter who made her very proud. She was the only one she had sent for who left the country. For some reason, Jean and Ernst never made it; they got denied multiple times. A few years after her daughter joined her, they managed to build a house. That house was fifteen minutes away from my grandmother's, and Jean and his official family occupied it. That house was not as big as my grandmother's; it was just unique with three bedrooms, a living room, a dining room, and a kitchen. There was a bathroom out back, two storage places, and a garage as well. The first storage place was used as a *boutik*, an area used to sell goods, especially food. The other storage place was used to store vehicle parts. Jean had a side business where he would rent his truck to people who needed it the most when they were dealing with construction, or when they were moving some heavy equipment. From my understanding, whatever my godfather owned was not from working hard. They were all given to him by his mother or his cousin Daddy.

I remembered when I first met Cleante. She was not as excited as my grandmother was. I was a bit older around that time, and she looked at me and waved "Hi."

I waved back with a welcoming smile trying to get her to say something to me, but that did not work. She was quiet, as always, and she was wearing a long dress with red and white stripes. She was not much of a talker; she sat there, enjoyed the food Yaya had cooked for her, talked about some family stuff and how different things are in America. I remembered one thing she said about me since my mother never had me to visit the country in which I was born. Cleante blurted out, "If he were in his country, he'd be way bigger."

She rarely visited the house I grew up in, and when she did, the whole house became as silent as a cemetery…that was how humble she was. Whenever she came back to visit her country, she never stayed in the home she and her daughter built. During the daytime, you might have seen her in there only if Jean was around, but she never slept there or stayed there long enough. As I grew up, I realized the reason she was not too happy about staying in her own home…you do not want to be a burden to a whole family. She usually stayed with her neighbor, Ms. Virgine. She and Virgine had an unbreakable bond, but I was not so fond of Virgine just because she lied about me doing something, which got me in big trouble. Aside from that, she was a cool neighbor. She lived by herself, and I guess it was a nice gesture from Cleante to keep her company. Her house was beautiful except she turned her backyard into a farm. During their free time, which they had a lot of, they would go to the little farm and feed the chickens and the hens, check if the chickens had laid eggs, and take care of the plants and plant some more. Ms. Virgine was the one who taught me a little bit about farming. There was a vast land owned by some wealthy old man not too far from her home. She would ask for his permission to use it and grow her corn. That was my first time farming, and it was awesome. Both Cleante and Virgine were my instructors, Cleante being the cool one, Virgine, not so much. She was pretty mean.

"Your job is to dig holes just like I showed you. Do you think you can do that?" Virgine would tell me with an authoritative voice like she wanted to let me know she was the boss.

She knew I was doing a good job because not only was I following her footsteps by not digging the holes too deep, but I also put in the green ruler to measure the depth of the hole and the inches they were supposed to be from each other.

I would have a creepy smirk on my face whenever Aunt Cleante went, "He's a big boy; he knows what he is doing. He'll be fine."

There would be a huge ball of fire in Ms. Virgine's eyes as sweat went down her chin and she said:

"Don't do that to him."

"What is it? What am I doing to him?" said Cleante.

"This! You are softening him up. You have to toughen him up."

"Toughen who up? He's just a child. He is only six years of age!"

"Exactly my point. You have to start from there to make him the man he's supposed to be."

"I think you are overreacting. Jenkins, honey, you are doing just fine. Keep it up."

That grin grew larger on my face as I thanked Aunt Cleante and said to Virgine with a childlike voice, "Look! I am doing fine just like auntie said. My holes look exactly like yours except mine are more circular!"

She did not congratulate me. Instead, my aunt gave me a look that almost made me cry. I remembered feeling a bit down, as I was trying to prove myself to someone I admired at the time. As I was digging holes under the meanest sun you could think of, sweats were making their way from my forehead down to my heels, and my eyes were like a balloon filled with water and ready to burst at any moment.

Sadness hit home as Ms. Virgine called out my name loudly and went, "You are not going to cry now, are you?"

I kept my head down so my tears would water the soil and to not embarrass myself in front of the humblest person who happened to be my great-aunt.

"No, I'm not," I replied in a trembling and shy voice.

"Look up, young man. The soil is not the one talking to you. I am."

I still kept my head down as my auntie went, "Come one now, cut him some—"

Ms. Virgine quickly interfered by saying, "Cut him some of what? Come here young man. Look up. At least if you are crying, cry like a man and look at me right in the eye while doing so, and Cleante, please keep away."

I slowly lifted my head and took a good look at the sky. Not that I wanted to look at the clouds, but because I did not wish the tears to drip down my cheeks. I finally had my eyes on her. We stared at each other for quite some time, and no tears came out. It was like she was waiting for me to cry some more before she could spit out some words. I tried my best not to let any more water escape my eyes. She got the best of me. At some point, I could not hold them anymore. I allowed the tears to run, and I cried like a baby. Nasal discharge ran down my chin, cries of an innocent baby covered the whole neighborhood, and lots of tears made sweet love to my cheeks, making me a new, watery necklace.

"That's it, little guy," Virgine said, "Let it all out, and keep your eyes on me."

In my mind, I was like, *You will have to stay here all day for me to let it all out because I got plenty more where those tears originated.*

Virgine finally approached me and kept looking straight at my watery eyes and blurted out these exact words, "Look, young one, there will be times where you will need those tears. They might come out, they might not. Fact is, you have to let those feelings out however form they show up. Do not be ashamed of crying. That's just a taste of how life gets, and trust me, young one, it will get harder."

I did not know how to answer this, and I replied by saying: "Thank you?"

She looked at me all surprised and said, "Is that how you are going to say it? How about you say it like the man I know you are. Can you try that?"

Cleante tried to interfere, but she did not get the chance, as Virgine stopped her.

I looked right in her eyes and stood like a soldier while keeping my right hand up to my head in a soldier salutation form and yelled out, "Thank you, Ms. Virgine!"

That was the first time I had seen Virgine smile, and I smiled too.

She then turned her back to me and said, "That is more like it, young one. Now wipe those tears away and keep up the good work."

That good feeling started to come back as I was wiping the river and grin off my face.

Ms. Virgine came back with her serious face and knelt before my little body, then went authoritatively, "Now stop digging. You have dug enough."

I thought that was my cue to leave and go take a shower and eat. As I was leaving she yelled out, "Hey! Come back here; you are not done yet. Now take that bucket of corn kernels and put three of them per hole."

There were many holes to dig, for it was a vast land. I did not dig them myself. We all did it together. Part of me wanted to keep working, but at the same time I needed a break. Sadness sort of hit home again as I took the massive bucket of corn kernels and got ready to put in some more work. I remembered Great-Aunt Cleante looking at me, smiling as the sun was grilling my face. I remembered the conformity that came with that smile and the amount of courage it gave me that day to keep on putting corn kernels into the holes I had dug.

"It looks like you need some help with that, Jenks," she said to me smoothly.

I was scared to accept her offer because I did not want Ms. Virgine to be mad at me, and I respectfully rejected her offer. That was the worst decision I have ever made. Here she came again, Virgine, with a meaner face this time, and she blurted out, "How are you going to reject such a nice lady's aid? Remember what I've told you. Act like a gentleman, and think about making another decision."

I looked back at Cleante and smiled. My heart was filled with joy as she was headed my direction.

I then said, "Please, Auntie, can you help me now?"

She looked at me, placed both of her soft hands on my little cheeks, which left a great amount of dirt on my face, and then she kissed my forehead and said, "It'd be my pleasure, dear."

We planted corn until the sun cooled down a bit, and after such hard work, we went to Ms. Virgine's house for some *Soup Joumou* and a nice shower.

There was one thing Ms. Virgine was right about, and I was not too fond of the fact she was right. That was the lesson she taught me about crying. That would be my biggest challenge to come, and it would become the worst experience anybody could ever endure. During this tough moment, I had no choice but to be as humble as that disguised stranger, My great-aunt Cleante. That is how I think the world should be: humble, worry-free, no need to make things harder as life already is. As I was walking down the bumpy roads to fulfill my destiny in life, those three sisters helped me through the hard times. I have to say all three of them changed my ways for the better, as I was destined to be a witness to a tragedy that was a bit easier for me to deal with by their teachings.

PART I

HELL

Chapter Five

Welcome to Hell

Just like it stated in the Bible, there is one God who is manifested in three persons. That is how I saw myself. I saw myself as one human being who had been transformed into three different persons as I was moving from neighborhood to neighborhood. Each community has given me a chance to look at life differently, and all of them have granted me the opportunity to express the hidden personalities I had within myself.

My second life has been broken down into three neighborhoods with the third being the most important one. That was where the tragedy that would change my ways took place. Most people would agree a community plays a huge role in a kid's life; it will shape who they are to be in the future. To me, this is not entirely true, for I am living proof. I believe we all decide whom we are going to be. It does not matter if the neighborhood was good or bad. It does not make a difference if you had good or bad parents. We are the captains of our ships. We set our destinations and follow the paths that are best for us.

I have been blessed to have such a mother figure (*Yayoo*) who allowed me to be whom I wanted to be. One sure thing is no matter how good you raised a child, at some point in that child's life he will make some mistakes, and there is nothing you can do to prevent that from happening, and that was my case. I have had my fair share of errors, and the good thing is I have learned from them, but there is one of them from which I did not learn anything at all. I have ignored it until it stopped existing for a while. I have locked it in a box and thrown it in the depth of the ocean where it could no longer be found, but that did not stop it from coming back. I thought throwing it away would mean it never existed in the first place, but the truth was, doing so would make it remain one of the mysteries of the world.

The first neighborhood was in Carrefour, Mariani, but we called it "*Ti Source*" which means "little river" because that neighborhood was known for that river. That was where I spent most of my childhood, and it is the one where my childhood homes came into existence. This neighborhood, I named it Hell not because it was the harshest one but because of the type of personality it brought out of me. My grandmother's house was in this neighborhood, and this is the exact neighborhood I have described before as a Tintoretto's painting. This home was located in the middle of a long line of other houses. It was facing the little river. The main road separated the small stream and the other businesses that were going on at the time from my childhood home. To get access to the river, you had to go down a hill. Not that the house was built on a mountain, it was more like someone had dug a huge hole, and from there the little river was born, and that would create the illusion of the house being on a hill. If you were to go to Cleante's house or go to the capital where the government's palace was located, the house would be on your right. To the left would be the little river, of course, and the long line of private businesses, mostly boutiques and people sitting on the side of the street trying to sell some stuff.

From the upstairs balcony, where we used to sleep, you could spot the little river clearly and the big oak tree. You could see the green mountains and the beautiful reddish sky when the sun sets. You could also see the soccer field—not much of a soccer field. It was just a vast land where my friends and I used to play soccer from time to time. That land was about two minutes away from the house, and that place was like a second home to me. You had to cross the river to gain access to it. If you had the eyesight of a seven years old, you could also spot the *Mariani Maché,* that was a supermarket that was in the heart of Mariani. That was a thirty to thirty-five minute walk from the house, and that was where Yaya used to buy fresh produce and other cooking goods. You could also spot the sea and some of the boats sailing because the sea was not too far from the supermarket. Standing on that balcony felt like being the king of the neighborhood. You had eyes over pretty much everything that was happening. It felt like I had Hell on the tip of my fingers.

I have associated *Ti Source* with Hell because that was the neighborhood where I had my worst experience as a child. I was the only kid living in this big house. It got boring sometimes in there, and that meant I had plenty of time to think and come up with something stupid. Apart from going to school and church with my aunt, I was not allowed to go outside to play with the other kids. That was tough on me. As time went by, I figured out different ways to sneak out and go wild. I remembered when I was five years old, it was the last day of class, and I also remembered feeling so excited. I could not wait to get home and set my cousin's wardrobe on fire. That was one of the worst mistakes I've made. It was intense, and part of me knew I had done something terrible, but I did not know I would have to pay the price. I always got very excited during the first day of summer vacation. It was still the same thing every summer vacation. I would have to stay home with my aunt and cousin and watch the other kids getting ready to go spend their summer vacation in the countryside to visit their grandmothers and other family members. After the first day of summer vacation, I always felt like I did not belong anywhere; it felt like I had no country of origin.

Those were the loneliest days, a whole three months inside not being able to go outside and play with the remaining kids, the ones who chose to stay and enjoy the hot summer days bathing and fighting in the little river. All I was able to do was stand in the balcony and watch them enjoying their summer while mine wasted away. Sometimes my aunt would send me to my godfather's home so I could be around his kids, and that was where I had met Ms. Virgine. I got home from school that day, and as soon as I entered the front door I already had a sense of what the summer would look like. I had to spice it up this time. I did not even take my uniforms off; I went straight to the kitchen downstairs, grabbed a box of matches, and went straight to my cousin's room. That was not my first time playing with fire, but this was the first time where it got real. I remembered burning the tablecloth with which my aunt used to cover her old sewing machine. Those were small fires, not as big as the one I started in my cousin's room that day. I stood in the middle of her room, scanned for the best item to set on fire, but could not find any. The tablecloth was lame now; I wanted to challenge myself. I wanted something big, something spectacular. I was dying to put on a show and make that summer something to remember.

Finally, my eyes fell onto her wooden wardrobe. That closet spoke to me that day. That closet wanted to be burnt by no one else but me. I approached the wardrobe and tapped it a couple of times. I examined it with care to find a little creek to drop the burning match. I could not find an open spot, and the closet seemed impenetrable. Never give up on anything: That was what I learned that day. As soon as I was about to abandon the mission, I slapped the closet's door with such rage, and voila! The door was not even locked; the wardrobe itself allowed me to pursue my dream.

I lit several matches until my dream came true.

I remembered seeing the beautiful, yellow flames dancing inside the closet and the gray smoke hugging the ceiling.

I did that.

That was what I was thinking as the flames grew and the fumes cheered all around me. At some point I realized what I had done, and that was when I heard some of my great-aunt's friends who were sitting on the balcony that was connected to the staircase yell, "*Yayoo! Dife!*"

Within seconds, Yaya made her way upstairs past the hallway and into my cousin's room. She made her way through the heavy smoke while she was yelling out my name. She finally saw me lying down in a fetal position as I was trying to breathe. She scooped me up and brought me outside to the balcony. I have never seen such disappointment in someone's eyes before. I could feel I let her down that day. My actions did not affect the way she cared for me. Even though I almost burnt the whole house down, I could still feel her love. She hugged me and asked me if I was okay. She kept checking my body for burns and my eyes as well. There was no fire station nearby; my aunt and her friend put out the fire as she ordered me to stay out on the balcony.

I stayed there for almost an hour, and I did not think I was going to get punished for what I had done considering how my aunt approached me after such a scene. After they managed to put out the fire, Aunt Yaya checked on me again, but this time with a new type of smile. I could not tell if she was trying not to smile or if she was trying her hardest not to make me feel bad about what I had done, but I did not really like that new smile.

She came at me and went, "Roro…you have done an awful thing. People could have been hurt, and you could've been hurt."

A hug followed as I stayed quiet, and then she blurted out, "I do not have the strength to punish you for what you have done, but you will have to pay for it."

I thought there was no way she could punish me; she loves me; she will go to her room and work on her dress or go out with her friends. That was not the case. She went downstairs to make a phone call.

She was on the phone for quite some time, and as I grew bored upstairs, I went downstairs and caught a glimpse of the conversation where she went, "Do not be too hard on him. That is his first mistake."

I had goose bumps all over my body as I heard the bad news. I did not know to whom Yayoo was talking on the phone, but whoever it was, I was going to get a great ass-whooping from that person. From this moment, I was starting to regret the perfect decision I had made. I began to cry and asked my aunt to forgive me. I assured her it would never happen again. She told me it was too late for that now. My fate was sealed, and I was destined to get that ass-whooping that day. Not too long after she had that conversation with me, I heard a loud knock on the front door. I quickly ran upstairs, as I thought it was whomever my aunt had called. I was hiding under my cousin's bed in the room smelling like burnt sheets. I remembered hearing the big, scary voice of my godfather, Jean, asking about my whereabouts. I was shaking from under the bed, and I tried my best to stay quiet as tears were running down my cheeks.

"Come on downstairs, honey. You will only make things worse for yourself," Aunt Yaya yelled.

I did not answer. I was still under the bed hoping my godfather would get bored and decide to leave. A whole half hour had passed, and he had not asked for me. I thought he probably forgot about me, but the whole reason why he was here in the first place was to teach me a precious lesson. I thought I was off the hook as I was making my way out from under the bed. As I stuck my head out, I saw his first dog, Beethoven. The dog started barking at me, and suddenly the big, scary voice came back.

"Jenkins! *Vinn jwenn mwen.*"

To those who do not know what this means, in the Haitian culture, whenever someone calls you out like that or uses a sentence precisely like this one, that means you are in trouble. It was like magic; I felt compelled to move from under the bed and go down the fifteen steps as

Beethoven was following me. It was like he was cheering for my godfather. He was supporting him in whooping my ass that day. As I made it downstairs, I saw the tall, big, and scary-looking Godfather Jean standing in the living room with a belt in his hand.

"I heard you are burning things in here. Is that true?" he said with a deep voice.

"Yes, it is, but—"

"No buts. You do not get to say anything else. You already admit you did it. What do you think I should do to you?" he asked me as he was rubbing his belt

"Whoop me with that belt?" I said to him as I was crying

"Oh no, you don't get to choose your punishment. I got a surprise for you, young man."

"What is it?"

"It will not be a surprise no more if I told you what it is. Now fetch me the box of matches you used to burn the wardrobe, young man."

As scared as I was, I had no choice but to obey to everything he said. I knew he was not going to use the belt, which was right in a way, but I did not know what he had in store for me. I was thinking maybe he was going to use the box of matches to teach me a lesson about not using it anymore, which in a way he did, but not the way I envisioned it. I went straight into the kitchen and grabbed the box of matches and brought it out to him. He ordered me to sit down as he pulled the front curtains and allowed everybody on the street to witness what was going to happen. He started by asking everybody outside this one question as I sat quietly waiting for him to start his show.

He asked them, "What happens when you play with fire?"

They all answered joyfully, kids and grownups all together, "You get burned!"

At this point I was thinking, *Well...that was easy, now can I go upstairs and play with my toys.* That was not the case.

Jean turned to me and said, "You heard what happens when you play with it. You get burned, kid. Now give me your index finger."

I did as he ordered, and he held it tight. He told me to keep it still as he lit one of the matches from the box.

He looked at the crowd outside while he was holding the burning match and went, "Let this be a lesson to all of you kids who like to play with fire. You do not want to know this feeling." He turned back to me and asked if I was ready.

I was as confused as the dog watching the whole show. I did not know what he was talking about, and before I could open my mouth to say anything, he already put out the well-lit match on the knuckle of my index finger.

"Now you know exactly how the wardrobe felt when you set it on fire," he said to me as I was crying and holding my index finger.

Some of the kids outside were laughing. Some of them did not even care, but a couple of them were crying along with me. Those were the ones I saw setting their notebooks on fire. I asked them if I could do the same thing, and they responded affirmatively, but I took it to a whole new level. Instead of burning my notebook, I did my cousin's wardrobe. That was the beginning of the *Troubled Jenkins*. This was my first dark day in Hell, and that summer was one for the books.

In this neighborhood I was what you would call an "asshole," an ignorant, and a bully. I grew not to care what anybody thought about anything, and I was sort of reckless but not in front of the grown-ups. Everything would take a turn for the worse when my godfather's kid was sent to my aunt so she could raise him too. A new kid in the house, of course, I was going to show him who was boss around here. Stevenson was his name, and this was where the worst part of his life began.

CHAPTER SIX

HELL'S PERKS

It must be puzzling for a mother, for any mother, to have to leave her child behind due to a situation. That was the state in which Stevenson's mother had found herself. Such a beautiful woman she was. She had very long, dark, silky smooth hair. She was tall with sparkly eyes and a bowlike set of lips. She was as light as my grandmother, and she was the real definition of a true Creole woman (*Vrè fanm Kreyol*). Stevenson was her first child. She had two others, a daughter and another son. The truth was the father of the other two kids did not like having Stevenson around, not because he was a reckless one, but only because he was not his son. His mother had no choice but to come to our house and leave Stevenson into my aunt's loving arms. The moment I saw Stevenson, I was surprised and confused. My whole life, I had been the only kid living in this house, and now there was another one. I was sort of happy, but at the same time I did not want another kid to steal the love my aunt had for me. I was not ready to share that love.

I was upstairs watching television when they entered the house. I had no idea we were going to have visitors that day, and if I knew, I would have worn something different. I remembered having on Cookie Monster shorts and no top. It was early in the morning, I just had breakfast, and I was entertaining myself by watching gospel cartoons on channel four. I rushed downstairs to spend some quality time with my aunt, and there he was, a young boy, much younger than me. He was probably around six or seven years old, and I was about nine or ten years of age.

The moment I saw him, I remembered asking myself, *Who is this? What are you doing here? What's your agenda?*

As I was asking myself those selfish questions, Stevenson ran towards me and grabbed my right hand and smiled.

I recalled the joy on both ladies' faces as Stevenson's mother blurted out, "Would you look at that. They are getting along already."

I was not the smiling type of kid. I stood there looking as mean as I could as Stevenson was still holding my right hand while smiling.

As soon as I was about to pull my hand away from his, my aunt sensed I was going to do something stupid and told me, "Roro, why don't you be a good boy and give your new brother a tour of the house."

I was stunned by the fact that my aunt said this kid was my brother, and immediately I asked her, "How is he my brother? I've never seen him before, and he looks nothing like me."

Stevenson's mother laughed hysterically at my response. I ended up laughing too because her laugh was sort of funny.

My aunt proceeded by saying, "Well, young one, do you remember the guy who taught you the lesson about playing with fire? That is his son."

Frère de baptême would be the perfect way to describe Stevenson's relation to me, but I call him "cousin." In the Haitian culture, whenever someone baptized a child, that person's kid automatically became the child's Godbrother or Godsister After hearing such news, I took Stevenson upstairs and started to show him around. He was amazed. I could tell he loved the house, and most importantly, he loved being around me as well. I asked him how much he knew about his father.

He gave me a shoulder shrug and said, "I do not know him at all."

One thing was on my mind for sure as I was showing him around, revenge. I wanted Jean's son to pay for all the ass-whooping he gave me back in the days, but it turned out my godfather just got an extra pair of fresh new asses to whoop now. Being the only kid in a house that big was one thing. Now bringing another child to join that lonely kid, you can only imagine how chaotic it got sometimes. We became inseparable. Everything we did, we did it together, even getting our ass whooped by his dad.

We both grew up in this neighborhood I associated with being like Hell. I would become a different type of person, the one who traumatized and manipulated Stevenson for days. It all started during the bullying season at school. I was not the type of kid to defend myself in any situation. I used to get bullied a lot in school, and the reason behind it was because I was what most Haitians would call a *"Rechinya"* or *"Ti Kriye."* That was how we referred to someone who liked to cry a lot for no reason at all. That was me. I was a sympathetic kid growing up. Anything you said or did would result in hurting my feelings, and I had a hard time coping with that in school. The problem was not me being bullied all the time. The real issue was the fact every time I came home from school Stevenson was the one to pay for everything that happened to me in class. I had been bullied from the third grade to sixth grade. Sometimes it would happen when I reached the higher grades, but not as often as it used to. I had become Satan himself when it came to mistreating Stevenson. I don't want to be sorry for all the things I did to him because I do not want to think being sorry would fix it. There is no way to fix something that terrible. I made his childhood his Hell, and to balance that, I dedicated the rest of the days I have to live to relive these exact horrible moments, to remind myself of the type of monster I used to be. Some actions cannot be forgiven, and some of them cannot be forgotten.

Stevenson was and still is the most influential person I know. I do not think anybody would have the strength to survive the things I did to him. That was the neighborhood where I became the thing I hated the most. I became a bully. That was the neighborhood where I first fell in love. At least something great came out of it. Not too far from the house lived a kid, a very reckless kid, named Stanley. He was an evil kid, and he introduced me into some bothersome stuff. I knew him way before Stevenson came to us, and Stanley was known for his incredible fights. I guess in a way I was his Stevenson because he used to bully me as well. He'd pick fights with anybody, older kids, grownups, even dogs. He was not my friend. He was more like a companion, but I liked having him coming over when my aunt was not around so we could play with marbles (*jwe mab*). My aunt was against playing with marbles. She thought the idea of playing with marbles (*Mab*) would make one a sick kid (*Vakabon*), or a naughty person. The concept of the game was to bring a fair amount of *Mab*, so does your opponent. We would draw a circle on the floor and place all of them in. We would then draw a line a couple of feet away from the ring containing the marble, and this was where we were to shoot with one marble and take out as many as possible from the circle.

Stanley was pretty good at this game, and he would be the reason I realized why my aunt was so against playing the game. Some people would put a few coins instead of marbles inside the circle. When money was involved in a game, it changed the intensity of it. The game lost its fun part and become a bit dangerous. Sometimes I would watch from the balcony Stanley playing with money and end up beating the living hell out of the person who won. Sometimes he would sneak around his opponent and take all the money and make a run for it. Most of the time they would catch him and give him a beating, but he did not care about that.

He was not afraid of his mother even though she was more stringent than his father. His father he feared for some reason; I did not understand why. I remembered the first time he helped me sneak out of the house to go to his. Not too far from his home were the woods, but a mile from the woods was a little pond, not a popular one. As I sat in his living room, all bored, he suggested we go for a walk in the woods, so I agreed.

He took me there and asked me, "Have you ever seen a lady's private part before?"

I was stunned by this question. I did not know what to say, but I tried to let some words out of my mouth by saying, "I am not supposed to see that, man, it is bad!"

He fell on his stomach. I thought he tripped on a rock, but it turns out he did it on purpose. He was laughing so hard he ended up crying from doing so.

I stood there while he was on his stomach laughing away, waiting for his laugh to stop so we could continue our little walk in the woods. He was finally done having his laughter. He then got up and put his huge hands on my shoulders and went, "Look, this is all going to change today. I will make you a man today, my friend."

As a five-year-old kid, I did not know how to react to this. All I wanted to do was enjoy outside for a few minutes then head back home before my aunt got there. We kept on walking, and finally we got to the little pond where three girls were cooling themselves down under the angry sun. They were pouring water on themselves with all their clothes on. I had no idea things were going to change as soon as we got there. He seemed to know the girls, as he addressed them by their names, and the way they responded, it seemed like they knew him as well. They kept on conversing for a while, and it seemed like they were not in agreement with something he mentioned, as their mood changed.

"Hey, come a bit closer," he commanded me.

I did as he ordered, and he looked at me with the creepiest smile I have ever seen and said, "Do you want to see their private parts?"

Just by saying that, all three of the girls looked at me. They all looked very sad, and they were waiting for me to decide their fate that day.

I looked at him and said: "I told you already, I am not supposed to see that. It is not good."

He grew angry as I said that, then he started to rip up their clothes. I have never run so fast my entire life. I left him behind, and all I could hear were the girls screaming and his evil laugh.

Later that day, I snuck out again to check on him. I went to his house, but he was not there, and it seemed like his mother was also looking for him. Her facial expression told me he was in big trouble. As soon as I was getting ready to leave for my house, he showed up at the bottom of the front steps asking me if his mother was home. I answered positively to him as he tried to run away. I knew he was in trouble, considering what he had done earlier that day.

As he was trying to run away, his mother came up on the front porch and said, "Stan, baby…I've been looking for you all day. Where have you been? Have you eaten? Come on up; I have cooked your favorite meal."

I knew something was wrong because her mood changed so fast from being mean to the nicest mother ever.

Stanley did not seem to buy into her trick either for he said, "Mother, I know what you are up to. This is not the first time. If you are going to give me an ass-whooping, just get it over with, please. You know I do not like surprises."

His mother waved me goodbye, as a sign for me to not witness what was about to go down. I wanted to see how he was going to get his ass whooped.

His mother then said, "Come on up then, my boy. I know you'd figure that out. You are so smart, but not smart enough to leave those poor girls alone."

As he was making his way up the front porch, I thought his mother had a belt hidden behind her back, but that was not the case. She had one of these old Coca-cola bottles, the heavy ones, and she broke it right in his face, and his face turned red with a significant amount of blood.

It looked like he was enjoying it. He looked at me as blood was dripping from his face, laughing, and then he said, "My friend, you need to go now. You do not need to witness what is coming up next."

He was right. I wished I did not stay around to see what happens next. The whole scene looked weird to me. How could he enjoy such a beating? The mother was also laughing. Usually when my godfather gave me a beating I kept screaming for help, and sometimes my aunt would be behind the front door crying as I was too, but this one was the complete opposite. She broke another glass on his face, not a Coca-cola one, but a wine glass this time, and she pushed him off the porch to the street. He was lucky enough because there were no cars passing through at the time. He fell on his stomach just like he did it on purpose earlier to laugh at what I had said.

He looked back at me while he was bleeding on the street and went, "I told you not to stick around for this one, man."

I was not the only kid witnessing such a scene; there were dozens of other kids watching this. He got up, wiped his bloody face with his hands, and then wiped his bloody hands on a kid's face from the crowd that was watching him suffer.

His mother then came back, picked him up like he was a baby and said: "Now, baby boy, have you learned your lesson?"

He nodded, "Sure, Mother. I did just like the previous ones, and I love you."

His mother looked back at him while holding him and said, "I love you too, son, and this is why I am going to use lemon juice and rubbing alcohol to treat these wounds."

As she was going up the stairs with him, he looked back at me and said, "I will be fine tomorrow."

That was the sort of thing I witnessed in the neighborhood where it all began. The upstairs balcony was like a movie theater. I watched some good and some bad movies as well, and most of them were action ones.

Sometimes when we spent months without running water, the little river would be packed with people trying to get water to their homes. It was not like we have it here in America where we have running water 24/7. In Haiti, CAMEP is responsible for providing water for the community, but they do not offer that daily. In the house, we had a vast reservoir to store the water, and we also filled some containers as well so we did not have to go through the trouble of getting water in the river. I sort of love those days when it was packed in the river because I had to watch the most brutal fights. There would be punches, kicks, sticks, rocks, machetes, and sometimes large bricks involved.

One particular and most important thing that made this neighborhood my Hell was the separation of two loving sisters, Yaya and Ana. I never thought that was even possible. Even though they had their differences, you could still spot the love that existed between the two. That would be the reason why the second neighborhood would come into existence.

Chapter Seven

Conflicts and Vices

There is nothing worse than for a man to watch the two women he loves the most fight each other. For some people it could be their sisters or cousins. For others it might be their mother and wife or girlfriend, and it might also be two girlfriends. My case was different. Watching my aunt and my beloved grandmother going at each other unlocked the hidden gate of Hades that was inside of me. I never thought something like that would ever happen; it was a bad situation and one that kept me up all night wondering which one I was going to side with after the whole scene. I remember that day like it was yesterday. It was a Friday night around 7:00 P.M. when my grandmother came around in a black SUV her driver parked in front of the house. It was usually my godfather dropping her off since they were practicing voodoo together, but they had a falling out, and she had to get someone else to drive her around. I could still hear the loud knocks on the front door, and I loved to open the door whenever it was my grandmother who was the one on the other side of it because as soon as I opened it for her a hug followed and a couple of kisses on both cheeks.

That night everything was backward. It was as though my eyes were in the back of my head, and I could not see anything straight. I opened the door all happy and in the hope of feeling those lovely arms wrapped around me, but they were not. Instead, they pushed me out of the way to create some space for love to escape right by me. I was shocked, upset even, but not as shocked as I was when I realized she did not even bother to say hi to Yaya. Yaya was sitting in the downstairs balcony (*Galeri*) and that balcony was facing the front door, so there was no way grandmother could have missed her. They always greeted each other and talked about anything that happened to them during the day, but that Friday love escaped. As my grandmother did not grant me my hug and the kisses, she went straight upstairs to rest.

Halfway through the fifteen steps, I said to her, "Grandma, is something bothering you?"

At that time, I was fifteen years of age, and I could tell when something was not right. My grandmother looked back at me and smiled that smile I could not resist. That was the last smile I had to enjoy from her, the only meaningful thing she'd left me.

As she turned to me with such a beautiful smile, she said, "*Ti Mireille,* some things you will—"

I quickly interrupted her by finishing her sentence for her by blurting out, "Some things I will never be able to understand? Is that what you are going to tell me? How about you try me? I am fifteen years old now. I'm old enough to understand life itself, so try me now."

She looked shocked as she came closer to me and whispered to my ears, "Some things, you will never be able to understand."

After those words, three pats on my back followed.

The worst night of my life started to form itself as my Yaya listened to her gospel music downstairs and my grandmother made her way upstairs. I never knew they were mad at each other. It did not look like they were. You had to be an expert at figuring out if someone was pretending to be okay or not to tell something was going on between the two. Considering all the troubles they went through during their youth, one would say this bond they had was just unbreakable. Since I could not get a clear answer from my grandmother, I went straight to my aunt and asked her the same question. It did not go so well, and I got the same answer.

At this point I was thinking, *What is wrong with grown-ups saying we, the young ones, would not understand what they are going through?*

I also could not help but think maybe if they explained to me what was going on, the whole fight could have been avoided. I still believe I possessed the power to change the situation that night, but this would be the reason I genuinely believe everything happens for a reason.

We do not always get the answers we are seeking. That night I wish I did, and this whole incident would be the cause of me leaving this perfect neighborhood to the second one I considered to be Purgatory. Not too long after my aunt gave me the same answer my grandmother did, her sister came back down, and that was when all Hell broke loose. I did not know who started the whole scenario, but it was not pretty. I was in a situation where I had no idea what to do. First, there was a pretty quiet arguing that was going on, then I heard the voices going up in flames, and before I knew it, it got physical. I tried to separate and got in the middle of the two of them, but I could not keep my balance as they were making their way outside. Yaya ordered me to stay inside as she was trying to help my grandmother up. I thought whatever they thought they were doing was over, but it was far from that as the men from the neighborhood got involved by trying to separate them. That was successful, but my grandmother did not go back to the house. She got back in the car, and her driver drove her back to her lodge.

When Yaya made it back inside, I greeted her with a hug, but she did not seem to enjoy it. That was the first time I had seen her being that mad, and it scared me a bit too that night. She did respond to my hug, in a way.

She stared right into my eyes and said those exact three words, "Pack your things."

Have in mind nobody had been kicked out by anybody. I did not hear anything like that. I was not ready to leave this neighborhood behind, and

I was not prepared to say goodbye to the house that made my childhood possible. I loved that house. More importantly, I loved it when my cousin, my aunt, and I were living under its roof. I had no idea this house would soon be deprived of its ability to breathe.

My cousin was not around to witness the whole thing, but the moment she came home, that was when the phones would not stop ringing. She called her father that night, Uncle Daddy, and she explained to him what had happened. Before we knew it, other family members and friends were calling to make sure everything was all right. It was the longest night of my life. Talking with my first girlfriend for the first time would be the second longest. It was impossible for me to sleep; sleep was nowhere to be found. My mind was all over the place, and I was wondering where we were going to live now. I had a tough choice to make, and I had to choose wisely. It was either I leave the house behind, my loving cousin, and my awesome grandmother, or I could stay and enjoy everything that house had to offer without my lovely aunt. That night, I even questioned myself this is not fair, I did not do anything to deserve such a punishment, but then it hit me. It was all about love, and love was all about sacrifices.

I tossed and turned that night, could not shut my eyes for a split second. Every time I did, I just saw the same situation playing itself over and over again. I did come up with a solution to this problem, but not until the next day. I figured it was possible to feel my grandmother's love from miles away; I did not need to be with her all the time, although, it was great having her around, her smile did bring me some comfort during my down times. I decided to move out with Yaya and start over again somewhere new, but where? I might've had a slight idea about where we were about to live since my godfather's wife left him in an empty house. It was a long day because we had much stuff to move, and the neighborhood in which we were going to live was about fifteen minutes away from the house. We had all the help we needed because my aunt was well-known in *Ti Source*. Some had offered their cars to make it easier for us, and some stayed behind and kept packing for us. The whole moving process took about three days to be over. The last thing I had to do, which was the hardest, was the fact I had to say goodbye to those sweet fifteen-step staircase.

This new neighborhood, Purgatory, was not too different from Hell. The only thing this new neighborhood taught me was to be more compassionate; it showed me how to be more sensitive towards others. In this neighborhood, I was surrounded by friends who went to the same school as me and a lot of talented and athletic people. Unlike Hell, this one was not too packed with private businesses. Instead, it was filled with people who go to work in the city and a couple of old women who sit in their houses all day trying to sell some goods. This neighborhood was quieter and way more fun. I had been in this neighborhood before as a kid. It was not new to me; this house was not new to me; this was where my aunt would drop me off after she picked me up from school so the "mermaid" could help me with my schoolwork. The mermaid was my godfather's wife. I called her a mermaid because of her beauty. She looked like one. At least to me she did.

I had no idea how my godfather managed to get his hands on such a beautiful angel. There were no words to describe her; she was a lost angel on earth and possessed everything you were looking for in a woman. She was intelligent, compassionate, patient, respectful, and she always took her time to listen to what you had to say no matter how old you were. She respected your opinion. I had never seen her unhappy; she was always smiling and always singing with her angelic voice. She loved to dance, and sometimes I felt like dancing with her, but I had two left feet. I remember watching her with such joy dancing with her daughters and sometimes with my godfather. I would sit on the front staircases with both my hands on my cheek and smile as they were moving slowly to the sound of the radio. I would spend a few hours there in this house because my godfather's daughters went to the same school as me at that time and got our homework done together.

We would be out of school around 1:00 P.M., and sometimes the older daughter would pick us up and walked us to the house. I would settle there, change my uniform, and put on the clothes my aunt dropped off for me there in the morning. We would eat very tasty food, and after the meal it would be time for us to start studying, and this part I hated with a passion. I hated it not because I hated school or schoolwork, but because it was kind of chaotic. I was not particularly eager to memorize anything.

As a second grader, I remember we had to memorize much stuff, especially poems. I remember a specific poem titled: "*Cantiques de Noel*" from a grammar book I hated so much. I remember having trouble memorizing this poem. The younger daughter had no problem learning it, but to me it was like trying to fit a potato into a Coke bottle. Whenever I was having trouble memorizing those poems, I could not help but cry, especially when the younger daughter already memorized hers, and then she got to go outside and play or ride her bike. As I was having trouble learning the poem, I had to watch the younger daughter having fun. I am not going to lie, that was painful to watch, and then I could not focus. I just wanted to be with her, outside having fun as well. I was not allowed to go outside until I got the whole poem right. I would cry my eyes out; I would cry so hard my cranium would feel like it was on fire.

It would feel like the whole world was on fire whenever I had to face those situations. Luckily, I had the mermaid to help me during those hard times, and for that, I was and still am genuinely grateful. She was very patient with me, sometimes more patient with me than her daughters. Sometimes she would put me on her lap trying to calm me down while my tears were soaking into her dress. She never showed signs of discouragement; she was always telling me I could do it and telling me to repeat after her. The mermaid was my hero, and if I can read and write today, she made that possible. My second godmother used to live with them as well. She sometimes would help me with my homework, but she was kind of tough, and she was not as patient as the mermaid was. My godmother was a big help in that house. I did not know what her relationship with the mermaid was, but they were super close. She would help with running the *boutik* and the other businesses the mermaid had going on at the time. The mermaid used to go to other countries to buy goods and come back to sell them in her own home. That was her job; she was a businesswoman, and a pretty good one too.

The mermaid was close to my aunt as well. She had much respect for her and was always asking her to stay a bit longer so they could converse some more. She would give her report on how I was behaving that day, and sometimes she would tell her I was a good boy even though I was not. She was gentle and was not the type to beat her kids. She left that duty to her husband, my Godfather Jean. My godfather was not around much, only during the night. He would spend his whole day outside with friends or some of his outside family, but on Sundays he would be there because that day was an exceptional day in this house. A typical Sunday would start with the whole family, except for Jean, going to church in the morning in a Catholic church located in a school named *"College Sacre Coeur Juvenat."*

Sunday morning would start by getting ready for church, but I was to get prepared in the old neighborhood and walked to Purgatory to meet with the mermaid's family. I usually watched everybody getting ready to leave, and sometimes I would help by zipping the back of their dresses, and putting on their bracelets or necklaces. If that were not the case, I would stay in the living room watching gospel cartoons, which helped me understand most of the subjects the priest was preaching. If my godfather was around, he would be the one driving us there. If not, sometimes we walked there, for it was not too far from the house. The mermaid's father would sometimes come to pick us up and drop us to the church. We would all dress to kill, looking like we were going to a very important event. There were vivid colors and the sweet smell of perfume all around me. The best part was yet to come, and this was the part I loved the most about Sundays. It was when we got to the church. We had to walk about two minutes to get inside the church. We were on the school grounds, but the church was a few meters ahead. The best part was the clacking sound the high heels and shoes were making as we were walking to make it to the church. It was all quiet, and all you could hear were the shoes conversing. Sometimes we would see peacocks walking around and dogs that were following us as we were making our way there.

I loved that church; the service was not too long, and everybody was on the same page. Unlike the Protestant churches, the one my aunt used to go to, the service was what we expected, and everybody in the audience was quiet when they were praying. I do not remember praying much; that was not my style. The way I prayed was just a simple conversation with God at that time.

I would ask Him, "How are you doing? How was your day? I would like you to allow me to have a great day today and watch over my family for me. Also, do not forget to help me be done with my schoolwork on time so I can go play outside with the other kids."

I would repeat the same prayer every Sunday, and that would change when I decided to go to my aunt's church. I always felt I did not belong there in this Catholic church, not because I didn't think I was the religious type, but because when it was time to get your communion, only the grown-ups were allowed to get in line and get the bread, but not the kids.

In the Catholic churches in Haiti, the priests used something we call "*Losti,*" which is a small piece of bread in a circular shape. I have always wondered what this bread tasted like, and I could not wait to be old enough or to be fully Catholic to get a taste of it. The wine, only the priest was allowed to drink. Later I would realize there wasn't going to be enough wine to give everyone else attending the mass. After the service, the mermaid's father would come back to pick us up and drop us back home. At my godfather's house, you could always tell it was Sunday. The day seemed different. The food they cooked was different, the vibe was different, and they had neighbors coming over to eat and have a great time. My godmother would be helping with the cooking since the business was closed on Sundays, and the mermaid would help us kids review our schoolwork so we had no problem reciting our poems in class.

◆　◆　◆

This house was where I had developed my first foul behavior, and it was not a good one. I could have been in big trouble growing up if my godfather did not teach me a lesson about it. At first, it started with small things, and then it grew bigger and bigger. I began to steal stuff from the mermaid's house and take them back to Hell with me. The first thing I ever looted was a toy gun. That toy gun was attached to a white teddy bear on top of a shelf. I was too short to reach such a tall ledge, so I used a chair, as I was looking around to make sure nobody was looking. I grabbed the teddy bear, ripped the gun away from it, and put it in my pocket. I could not wait until my aunt came back to pick me up so I could go to Hell and play with the lovely gun. It was not that I did not have enough toys with which to play, it was just I had never had a toy gun before. My aunt would not allow me to play with one. I stole it and only played with it when my aunt was not around. The thing about thieving was that you only get to enjoy your stolen stuff for a short amount of time, and I was not a good thief. I got so excited about that toy gun, I thought it turned me into a real security guard. I used to stay by the front door for a long time hoping someone would knock on it. If someone did, I would open and point the gun right at them. Some people would act like they were scared and let me pat them down, others would push me out of the way, but the point was I was having fun.

One beautiful afternoon, I would manage to make a huge mistake, something I never thought about and I should have. Whenever I had that toy gun with me, it took out all my troubles, all the sick times. I was living in the moment. Nothing else mattered whenever I had that toy gun by my side. As I was on duty that day, there was a notable knock on the door. Not a regular one, but I knew who had that knocking pattern, and he was the only one who knocked on the door like that. My mind, at that time, would not let me think straight as I had that toy gun with me. I heard *knock knock...knock knock knock...knock knock knock.*

I was so excited to point the toy at whoever was behind the door, but what I did not know was the fact the knocking style belonged to my godfather Jean. As soon as I opened the door, I pointed the gun at him, and that was the worst decision I have ever made in my life.

I had an ass-whooping that day. It turned out his mother, Aunt Cleante, had given him that teddy bear for his birthday, and he knew that teddy bear so well. He did not know who stole it, and he could not have figured out it was me because I was not tall enough to reach that high. The worst thing was the fact he did not even care about the missing gun. He already moved on about the whole thing, but I had solved his case for him. He whooped me greatly that afternoon. I remembered running in a circle as he was landing his huge belt nonstop on my butt. After the ass-whooping, I asked if I could keep the toy gun. At the time, it only seemed fair that after such a beating I should get to keep the toy. I believed I deserved to keep it. I had earned it the hard way then. That was not the case; he took it from me and asked me to go to the kitchen and grab him a box of matches. In my mind, I was confident I was going to get my index finger burnt again, but I went ahead while crying and got the box of matches. I gave them to him, and he lit one of them while he was giving me that evil look. He pulled the toy gun out and burned it right in front of me.

As the toy gun was reduced into ashes, he picked me up and said, "The next time you steal again, I am not going to burn whatever you take, I am going to burn your whole arm."

After scaring the hell out of me, he put me down and handed me fifteen dollars and told me to buy myself a toy gun. I did what I had always done with his money, just put them in my piggy bank and bought something nice for my aunt's upcoming birthday.

That would not be the last time I stole. I did it again. Not soon after I got caught with the toy gun, it was probably two years after my first unsuccessful robbery. This time, I aimed for something bigger, something that had value, something in today's world we cannot have a decent life in its absence. It was that very same thing that kept Haiti in the situation it is today because the only thing the government cared about was that thing of value. The people do not matter to them. Since the mermaid was a businesswoman and money was around, she became a target, and most people tried to rob her. That had become my new mission now, setting my cousin's wardrobe on fire being the first. That was what I was aiming for, the money. I was old enough to walk home by myself at that time; I did not need my aunt's assistance anymore. When it was time for me to leave my godfather's house, there was a vendor, an old lady who used to sell *fritay* (*frites*) on the side of the road, a couple of minutes away from the mermaid's home. That would be the reason behind me stealing for the second time.

That vendor was very nice, and for a vendor in Haiti she was way too sweet, and some people took advantage of her. Her cooking would make a full belly to develop the need to eat again. The smell of her frites was walking around the whole neighborhood and knocking at every door to invite people to take a bite from her delicious food. There would be a huge pot on her left side on top of three huge rocks, and in between those rocks laid the burning charcoals. There would be a pile of wood behind her to add to the fire to keep it alive, and because of that there would be a considerable amount of smoke leaving her tent and disappearing into the sky. In front of her there would be a large table with a rectangular-shaped, metallic container sitting on top. Inside that metallic container laid the result of her hard work. You could find fried plantain (*bannann peze*), fried sweet potato, fries, *akra, marinad, Griyo* and all types of other meat, but fried. There would be two bowls at the right of the metal-lic container that contained a very spicy kind of coleslaw (*Pikliz*), and the other one would be filled with some sauce, sometimes chicken or beef sauce.

I am not ashamed to say this old lady's food was the reason behind me stealing money now. When it was time for me to leave for Hell, I would first make sure nobody was around to see me doing such an evil act. Usually in the afternoon business was slow, and everybody would go outside by Ms. Virgine's house to sit and tell jokes or have a debate about the country's situation. That would be the perfect time for me to go inside the *boutik* and grab the can where they kept all the coins. I had and still have no idea where they used to keep the bills. I would not take too much money; all I needed was five "*goud*," which is a Haitian dollar. That was enough for me to get a decent amount of *fritay* and eat them on my way back to Hell. I would make sure I finished them before I arrived at the house because my aunt would question me about where I got the money to buy that food. Sometimes I would not finish it up, but I would save it until I got close to the house and give them to my neighbors' dogs. That would be the reason why they were so friendly to me and followed me everywhere I go.

I did not get caught as I did before with the toy gun. This time someone saw me and reported straight to my godfather. Jean did not burn my whole arm as he promised me two years ago. He did punish me shamefully. There was a house right next to his, and in between both houses was an alleyway (*Korido*). That alleyway led to a set of stairs, which led to another street called "*Impasse Jean Thomas*" that was parallel to *Rue Chez Cator.* I was crucified outside of Jean's house, but not the way Jesus was. On the wall that creates the alleyway with the neighbor's home, I had to mimic Jesus' position on the cross against it where everybody was coming from that alleyway. Not only I had to imitate the position, I had to do it backward meaning I had to face the wall with my face and my whole stomach making contact with it and both hands stretched as far as possible and with my feet crossed.

There were no nails involved, but I wished there were. Keeping my hands up there for an extended period was challenging. If I were to put them down, the impact of his belt on my ass would make me go back to the previous and correct form. Everybody was looking at the scene, children and grownups, and they were all laughing and picking on me. Some of them even tickled me to make me drop my hands; some were successful, others not so much. Out of all the taunts and name-calling shouted at me that day, only one stood out, and it was by a grown-ass man. As my head was turned to the right where the *Korido* was located, that man's eyes met mine.

They were watery, and he said, "Ladies and gentlemen, I give you Jesus Christ II."

After such a speech, laughter was born, and shame occupied my entire heart.

I did feel some type of way that day, but not too sad. I realized I was being punished for something I had done, but not for nothing. Some kids back in Hell, were being punished just because their parents were having a bad time. Compared to that I was treated fairly. I learned my lesson that day. When it was time for me to leave the cross, night introduced itself to the neighborhood. My godfather told me to go home, and this time there were no promises. I sometimes wondered was it because he knew I would change after such a punishment he did not say a word? Or was it because he knew no matter what he did I would continue to steal? I realized in the years that followed what went through his mind; he knew I would not go back to act like that anymore. That was a lesson well learned, a lesson well taught.

PART II

PURGATORY

Chapter Eight

Pre-Purgatory (Part I)

Eight years later, I found myself back to the same neighborhood, the same house in Purgatory. After such a hard punishment, I stopped going back to my godfather's home due to shame. Something else had happened as well, my grandmother spotted my godmother holding my shoulder from the back and kicked me on the butt with her knees. She thought they were mistreating me, and she did not want me to go there anymore, but she was playing with me that day. My godfather's wife claimed to have trouble with her eyes, and she would not be able to help me with my schoolwork anymore. That would be one of the reasons I stopped going over there, but the main reason was the shame.

Purgatory in its meaning is not a place; it is a process. If it were to be a place, the second neighborhood would be qualified to be called so. Purgatory is the process of purifying or cleansing your soul before you enter Heaven. It is the ridding of all the deadly sin you committed when you were living in your personal world. That was my case; it was not like I had a choice. I needed to be purified. I had to change my ways given the fact I had been doing a lot of stuff I was and still not proud of back then. At that time, I had the chance to change that; I had the opportunity to repent, not in a religious way, but willfully. It is a straight path when it comes to making it to Purgatory from Hell. There is a road separating both Hell and Purgatory from Heaven. If you were to keep on going all the way past Purgatory, you would have to keep to your left, then you will end up straight to the main road. On the other side of that road lies Heaven, which would later become my next destination.

I have come a long way from being Jenkins the abuser to being Jenkins the softhearted. I started to develop some new traits, and I developed a strange personality as well. I was around more mature people, grown-ups mostly, and more talented ones as well. My mindset was different, and now I could see both sides of the world and how unfair it could get. That was not the first time I had been to Purgatory as a teenager.

I used to go there to hang out with my other Godbrother everybody called "Bebi" who was in charge of the house since the mermaid had left. My godfather also baptized him, and that made us Godbrothers. After Jean's wife left him, he fell sick. His sickness was severe, and he had to stay in the hospital for an extended period. At that time, Bebi was the most responsible person my godfather could count on to take care of the house. The house was empty given the fact the mermaid took her business with her. I remember feeling bad for Jean because of the way he was living when his wife left him. I knew he was mean to me, but I do not believe he deserved what he got. That was when I realized something started to change within me, I should have been happy now that he was suffering, but I felt for him. I did believe he brought all of these things upon himself, which resulted in him being so sick, but no man should ever be feeling that way. Of course, he had other families out there, but this one was official. Not only was his family gone, but his marriage was in jeopardy as well.

His Hell would later become my Purgatory. I would go to this neighborhood around eleven in the morning and come back home in Hell around seven at night before the whole incident between the sisters. It was fine with my aunt as long as I kept calling her and let her know how I was doing. She could not tell me not to go over there. That would only push me to do so, for I was a reckless teenager. It was way more fun without having my godfather around.

Bebi would sometimes cook breakfast in the morning and save me a plate. He was not a very good cook, but he could make a tasty omelet and some Haitian-style spaghetti. Other than these two, he did not know anything about cooking a big Haitian meal. He would have several women coming over to take care of that for him. He had his way with women. I did not know his secret, but he was the man. I remember one girlfriend he had. She was light-skinned and she had freckles all over her face. They would taunt me as they were kissing. Bebi would turn around and look at me straight in the eye as his lips were swallowing his girlfriend's face.

Whenever he was done kissing her, he would turn to me and say, "You will never know what that feels like, little man."

My stupid response to that would be, "I hope I never do, considering the amount of spit you just swallowed."

I would later be the cause of Bebi leaving the house. He got kicked out. It was in December when Cleante came to Haiti because of his beloved son's condition. She did not stay in the house; she always stayed with Ms. Virgine even though the house had nobody occupying it at that time. Christmas time in Haiti was the time when most kids in the neighborhood would go away to spend the holidays with their grandparents. Bebi had planned to leave and visit his mother in Gonaives. That was a problem for me because I was not going anywhere, and with him around we were able to go in there and have a good time. We would tell jokes, watch movies, play cards and dominoes, and play video games as well. Now that he decided to go away for the holidays, I had to come up with a plan to gain access to the house when he was away. I tried asking him, but he did what any responsible person would do, he said no. I knew he was leaving in the morning, so I stayed over there up until 10:00 P.M. I waited until he fell asleep and went around the back and unlocked the kitchen door with the lock still on it so it looked like it was still locked.

That kitchen was never used. He used to cook in the backyard. He never paid any attention to that door.

I went home praying he would not notice the kitchen door was unlocked. The next day I went to the house to check if the door was still unlocked, and it was. That was all I needed, and the holidays would be a lot better now that I could get inside. The front gate was locked, but you could go through the neighbor's house, get on his roof, and jump down the backyard and you would be inside the house. Once inside, you could unlock the front gate and let other people in. That was how I allowed the guys with whom I used to hang out inside the house. There was the front gate, the one we used to let the cars in and out, and two other front doors we did not utilize. The middle front door was accessible when the mermaid was around, and once you got through the middle one, you would end up in front of a small staircase, and on top of it would be another door that led to the *Galeri*. We would spend days having fun in there without anybody noticing, but that upcoming Sunday was not our day.

Cleante knew the house was supposed to be empty and locked, but that day she would make a surprising discovery. I was playing video games with three other guys, including Stevenson. I played the game for so long I decided to head outside for a minute to get some fresh air. There was a huge truck parked in front of the house, and I was inside of it when Cleante discovered the front gate was unlocked. She did not see me because I ducked as soon as I saw her walk past the truck. When she realized the gate was opened, her mood changed, and she started to yell out Bebi's name. I knew Stevenson was going to get in trouble, but I also knew he was a smart kid, and he would find somewhere to hide from his grandmother.

Given the situation, I understood why my aunt was mad. She was not the type who would be angry, but that day I could tell she was enraged. It was understandable given the fact the son she loved so much was fighting for his life on a hospital bed. That was my first time seeing her like this, and that was the first time I saw this woman in such despair. She then proceeded to go through the front gate and then she realized the kitchen door was also open. She kept on calling Bebi's name, and still no answer. I saw her heading toward the kitchen door. Part of me wanted to yell out to warn the other guys inside, but I did not want to blow my cover. I did not want her to know I had something to do with it. Luckily, Stevenson was not the type to betray people. Cleante made her way inside the house where Stevenson told me he was hiding inside that old refrigerator, and the other two guys were running toward the *Galeri*, which was a stupid idea. From the truck, I could see them in the *Galeri* waving their hands, signaling me to come and help them by opening the door for them. I looked back at them and just gave them the middle finger as I was dying laughing then left the truck and went back to Hell.

After that day, I just stayed home until Bebi came back. I knew he would question me about the door being unlocked, but I did what I did best—I lied to protect myself. I told him I had nothing to do with it, and I was not even around when he was gone. He explained to me Cleante had talked to him about the two strangers she found in the house and she blamed him for leaving the kitchen door open. I just shrugged and told him I knew nothing about that and I was sorry for what had happened. Ever since that incident, the house was not that fun anymore, and Bebi was not the same person. That incident would be the cause of him breaking up with his freckled-face girlfriend, whom I did not appreciate. I knew all of this was made possible because of me. I was responsible for everything, but remember I was from Hell, and at that time I could not show any remorse or even feel sorry for anything. To me, it was like nothing had happened, and I was in desperate need for the house to be as fun as it was before.

Before the incident, everyone was happy, and the place was like headquarters for anybody to come in and have fun. In the morning, we would eat breakfast together, help my Godbrother to clean the house, and fill the reservoir whenever CAMEP decided to give us access to running water. In the afternoon we would all go outside, sit on the back of the pickup truck that was also parked in front of the house and check out the girls who was walking by us. Knowing the house was not too far from Ms. Virgine's, she could hear us talking and sometimes cussing. We would talk about girls all afternoon, but I usually stayed quiet because when it came to girls I knew nothing. Typically there would be the four of us hanging out, but sometimes some guys from *Impasse Jean Thomas* would come over to converse with us. Sometimes we would have a debate about the country and the political issues we were facing at that time. Most of the time it would be about women, and I learned some stuff I thought was impossible when it comes to dealing with girls.

"Pay attention, Kins, you do not want to end up like Guerlin," Bebi would say to me.

That would get under my skin, and sometimes I would leave them and go back to Hell to spend the whole day being angry at that particular sentence he blurted out. Guerlin was gay, and he lived a couple of miles away from Hell. I was so ignorant back then that I hated gay people just because they were being the person they wanted to be. I know for a fact Haiti's culture played a major factor in me feeling that way. In Haiti, gay people have no rights, at least at the time I was living there. Most of them spend their entire life in the closet. Only the strong ones like Guerlin and his crew had the courage to show their true selves. Guerlin was the nicest gay person I ever met, and whom I hated with a passion. He had a big house, and like my grandmother, he practiced Voodoo.

One day during summer vacation, I went to play soccer with a bunch of kids I barely knew. I was ten years of age at that time, and I had to sneak out of the house in order to join the kids. I was the one holding the ball as we were walking to the soccer field, not the field that was close to my house. I kept on tossing the ball up, but I was told not to do that just so the ball did not end up in someone's yard. I did not listen, and I kept on tossing it up. It was a scorching hot day, and I just had a fresh haircut, and sweat was dancing on my head and dripping down my neck. As we walked past Guerlin's house, I tossed the ball up and it ended up landing inside his house.

Guerlin was on his balcony enjoying some *Barbancourt* with his fellow gay mates. He saw the ball in his yard, and he stared at me in a way like he wanted me to ask him if it was possible to come and get it. At that time I was very homophobic, and rumor had it anybody who made it past Guerlin's front gate was considered fresh meat, and he would have his way with them. We all looked at each other, talking about who was going to get the ball back.

One of the kids yelled out, "He tossed it in there, why can't he go and grab it?"

Another one suggested, "Why don't we ask him if he could toss it back to us? That way we would not have to worry about entering his house."

Of course, I liked that idea, and I replied, "Yeah, let's do that instead."

The owner of the ball went ahead and asked Guerlin nicely if he could toss the ball back to us, but Guerlin seemed like he was waiting for us to ask him that question ever since the day he was born.

He would answer in the most feminine way. He had his left hand perfectly placed on his left hip and used his right hand to do a very loud snap as he blurted out: "I have broken my hip, and I cannot make it downstairs to toss the ball back to y'all, but you are more than welcome to come and get it. The door is open."

A weird smile escaped his lips as he said those words. The owner of the ball went ahead and tried to enter the door, but Guerlin interrupted him by saying, "No, I don't want you to come and get the ball. I have to pick...ooooh, this is going to be amusing. What do you guys think? Which one should I pick?" he asked his gay mates as they all looked around and checked us out.

Then they talked between themselves, and then a choice was made. Guerlin came back to the balcony with the same posture, pointed right at me and said, "You, you come and get that ball, young man."

I felt a cold rush coming from my feet to the top of my head. I tried to play dumb by looking around and tried to figure out whom he picked.

He then realized my dumb play and said, "*I chose you, you with the nice haircut, come and get the ball.*"

That was the longest walk I had to take. I was probably five steps away from the front door, but I made it there in ten steps while trembling and sweating. As soon as I was going to push the door open, Guerlin's maid pulled it open for me and said, "It is going to be okay, just go get the ball. It is under the car."

I was thinking, *Thanks lady, you have made it a lot easier for me to go through this situation.*

That lady was very nice and not very helpful in a way. In my mind, I thought not only was I inside his house, but now I had to bend over and grab the soccer ball. That was the toughest challenge I had to face at that time, but I completed the mission. I lay on my back and crawled under the car where my eyes met Guerlin's who was also reaching to get the ball on the other side. I froze as soon as I saw him. He took the ball and got up from under the car. I was scared to death, and I stayed under the car up until he ordered me to get up.

I did get up, and he handed me the ball and said, "I know you hate me; I know all my fellow Haitians hate me, but that is fine. At least I have to live my life the way I've always wanted to."

At the time, that did not mean anything to me. All I could see was a gay guy trying to convince me that was the way he was supposed to be living his life. I had a veil that was obscuring my view; I was not myself. In a way, I could say I was following society's footsteps. He had invited me to come upstairs where I would have the best time of my life. There was a party going on up there, and there were many girls in the living room where his little nephews were playing video games. He then proceeded by telling the other kids outside to leave as he tossed them the ball, and so they did. He had the girls feeding me, and I spent the entire day playing video games and eating exotic foods as he was still drinking heavy drinks with his friends. Before I knew it, word was on the street I entered Guerlin's house. Everybody knew what that meant, but only a few kids and I knew the real story. At that time, whenever someone compared me to Guerlin, I would get mad, I would be furious and wish I hadn't followed those kids to play soccer that day. Later on, that would be served as a moral lesson on how to accept people as they are. Unfortunately, Guerlin had passed, and I did not have the chance to tell him how sorry I was for seeing him the way I did, but at the end of the day, he was greatly accepted by me. I showed my acceptance to him by remembering how I used to see him and also by remembering such an experience I had with a friend I did not know I had at the time.

CHAPTER NINE

PRE-PURGATORY (PART II)

The time had come for Yaya and I to settle in a new environment. It was always a challenge to adapt to a new neighborhood, but this one, I already had a sense of it. I already know how it functioned. It was not too different from Hell. The only difference was between the houses. In Hell, I used to live in a two-story house, but in Purgatory, it was just a regular-sized house with three bedrooms, a living room, a dining room, and a *Galeri*. The *Galeri* was not too different from Hell's balconies, but this one you could see whatever was happening on the street. You could see Ms. Virgine's house and the blacksmith's workshop who used to work on the land Ms. Virgine and I used to grow the corns. The next door house that formed the alleyway (*Korido*) was my classmate's father's, and his son used to hang out with us too when my godfather was in the hospital. He was a bodybuilder, and he would later introduce me to lifting weights, something that ended up badly for me, considering how skinny I was.

The front gate and the other doors were replaced when we moved in, but the middle door was accessible this time. When you exit the front gate, you could spot another friend of mine's house. All you had to do was cross the street to gain access to his front door. There was no fence surrounded his home, but the *kandelam* trees were used as a fence for there were thousands of them. *Kandelam* is a small tree that spreads widely; it looks like a bunch of string beans all wrapped up on a stick. That tree comes in handy in Haiti. We use it as glue to fix damaged documents and bills as well. When you cut open a *kandelam*, there would be a white liquid coming out of it. That was what we used as the glue. If *kandelam* were money, my good friend Dave would be the wealthiest person in Purgatory.

His family was probably the most important one in this neighborhood. His father, the oldest guy in Purgatory, was a doctor. He practiced traditional medicine, and he would help deliver babies as well. His wife was selling goods and taking care of the house with the other kids. They had a two-story house, but Dave would build himself a room on the roof so he could concentrate more on his music. He built that room himself from scratch. Dave pretty much knew how to do everything himself; he was a handyman. He could play any instrument, and he also helped other kids to learn how to play them as well. His favorite instrument was the accordion. That was my favorite too, not that I knew how to play it, but because it gave the neighborhood a personal theme. He always played it in the afternoon around three. He would stand on the roof right next to his room and play it while singing and dancing at the same time. There would be people on the street looking and applauding him, and some would sing along with him as well. Sometimes I would be up there with him just watching him in sync with that accordion.

His father was as humble as my aunt Cleante, but kids hated him. I remembered hating him as a kid as well, but not as much as I hated my godfather. He was not a mean guy; we all hated him because of his profession. If you were a kid and you ended up in his office for treatment, you'd end up having the worst day of your life. He used herbs to heal people, and whenever some kids got hurt, he would be there to give them the meanest massage ever. We call that massage *"Rale"* or *"Manyen,"* but some people would come in to get a rubbing for fun. I do not know how you are going to pay that guy to give you a "*Rale*" just so you could enjoy it. Half of the people he gave massages to explained to others how painful it was. I would later realize why some of the grownups loved his rubbings.

I was once his patient. It was when the mermaid was still around, and I was probably six at that time. It was a Sunday, and the meal was perfect. They cooked country rice with black beans, beet and potato salad (Salade Russe), and there was also fish sauce. The fish was the reason I ended up under Dave's father's hands. It was a delightful day, as the food was so tasty, but the thing I had no idea about was the fact later on in my life, I would scan the fish carefully before I eat it. I was taking my sweet time to eat my food; the food was so good I did not want to eat it too fast. I wanted to savor it. I tried to enjoy it as slow as possible. That would be one of the reasons I ended up with his dad, the slow eating. As I was enjoying my food, I stopped eating for a while and started attacking the fish—Caribbean-spiced fish. I remembered almost biting my fingers off because of how delicious it was. After feasting on that fish, I went back to the rice and beans, and that was when I'd feel the little tingling sensation in my throat.

Every time I swallowed the food, I felt that sensation. At first I thought it was nothing; maybe it was how the food was making its way down my throat. Then it happened a second time, then a third, and so on. At some point I could not take it anymore, and I just started crying. There were tears everywhere, and my cry was in every corner of that house.

"What is wrong?" the mermaid would ask while she was running toward me.

My godmother replied, "He is probably crying for no reason again. You know how he gets."

The mermaid ignored my godmother and came straight to me and asked me what was wrong. At the time, I did not know what was going on with my throat; I did not know what to say.

I just looked at her and pointed to my neck and said, "I got ants biting me in here," as I was crying and sobbing.

The mermaid was a true mother; she immediately understood what was going on, so she told me to stop eating and avoid swallowing my saliva. I tried not to do that, but I got curious. I wanted to know if the sensation I was feeling was gone, so I kept on checking by swallowing just a little bit of saliva from time to time. Every time I did that the tingling came back, and the crying would start over again. She was gentle with me as she walked me to Dave's dad's house, and I would cough so hard to try to get that fish bone that was stuck in my throat out. It was the worst feeling in the whole world at that time, and I seriously thought I was going to die that day. The kids in the neighborhood boosted up that feeling when they started to pick on me.

We both got in his house, walked into what he called his office, which was the front porch, and he sat me down and told us to wait because he had another patient he was treating. That other patient was a kid with an injured arm. Rumor had it he fell off a two-story house while flying a kite. That was common in Haiti. Most kids died during Easter because of that. That kid was in much greater pain than I was, and I didn't want to be him that day. That kid would not stay still, and he kept on screaming. His screams made my crying stop for it was too loud. I realized there was no need for me to cry now. Nobody was going to hear me. The kid got all the attention in the world. Dave's dad strapped him up on the chair and left that injured arm unstrapped.

As Dave's father gave him the meanest massage on the arm on which he fell, the kid shouted out, "I AM FALLING, I'M FALLING! STOP NOW."

Have in mind this kid was strapped to a chair. That massage was so severe it made him think he was falling, but he was sitting still. After a few minutes of pure Hell and constant yelling, the kid finally passed out. It was quiet for a while, and now it was my turn to start crying again.

That kid quickly escaped his deep sleep to the smell of a solution that was stored in a bottle. I did not know what he was thinking, but as soon as he got back up from his sleep, he yelled out those exact words, *"LET ME FINISH!"*

Whatever he was doing while he was out cold, Dave's father should've let him finish it. The good news was his arm was all taken care of and he was free to go. The bad news was the fact I was next. The mermaid had left me there by myself and went on to take care of some stuff in the house. Before she left, she assured me everything was going to be all right. I wanted to believe her, but the thought of me dying that day was not going to leave my mind. Outside was packed with kids. It was like a concert with me being the rock star.

The crowd already knew my situation, so it was their job to make it worse. In Haiti, you would go crazy, literally crazy, if you paid attention or took anything anyone said seriously. You had to let it be and ignore it completely.

As I sat there swallowing bits of saliva just to make sure I was fine, one of the kids from the crowd was talking to another and said, "There is no other way to take that fishbone out of his damn throat. The doctor will have to slice his throat open to take it out."

As soon as I heard those words my mind froze, and it became clear to me that day was going to be my last one on earth. I jumped from the chair trying to escape his house, but I was not fast enough. I managed to make it to the front door, but the doctor's huge hands swept me up and brought me back to the front porch.

"Let me go! I do not want to die today! Let me go!" I yelled nonstop up until he strapped me up just like he did the kid with the injured arm.

At this point, I had no fight left in me. I gave up and waited for the doctor to decide whether or not I was to live or die this day. I was still shaking, and my tears were washing my entire face. As I sat there strapped on that chair, helpless, he came out with a butter knife, homemade bread, and a glass of water. The minute I saw that knife, I knew it, the game was over, I was destined to go out that way. All it took was a damn fishbone, and now my life was about to be over. Dave's father was not much of a talker. He was usually quiet, but he took his job seriously. As he approached me and sat down right in front of me on a chair he brought out himself, he put the butter knife on my lap and he called for his maid to bring him a jar of butter. At this point, with the knife still on my lap, I had no choice but to lie my way out of this situation, but what was going to be the best lie to convince him not to cut my throat? That was not easy for me to do considering I was not a good liar at that time.

That very same day, I would learn how to be the best liar ever. I did manage to come up with a lie, but it was not good enough. He figured it out. That was why he taught me how to be a good liar. He believed lying was an essential tool no one could ever survive in its absence. Everybody did it, and it made the worst situations a bit better, perfect even, if you had never been caught in telling one. He would say to me people would say lying was wrong and they hated liars, especially women, but the truth was they could not handle honesty. The lie was easily consumable. He would go on by saying the same person who was telling you they hate liars even forgot at some point in their life they've told a lie to get themselves out of a situation or to gain something out of it. Before he went on to give me such a lesson, I tried to convince him I was good to go and I did not feel that tingling sensation anymore.

I looked at him while the knife was still on my lap and said, "Sir, I am fine now. I can swallow my saliva without feeling anything. I'm all good. Can I leave now?"

"Is that right?" he replied, and I nodded affirmatively with a creepy smile that followed.

The maid finally brought up the jar of butter and put in on the floor right next to his chair.

He picked up the jar and finally took the knife off my lap, looked at me dead in the eyes, and said, "Do you even believe in the lie you just told me?"

He took the lid off the jar and scooped a small amount of butter with the knife and then he started to inspect my neck by running his fingers all around it.

"I do not believe it, sir."

He then picked up the homemade bread and said, "Why is that, little one?"

I said, "Because that lie is not the truth, and I only said that because I did not want you to cut my throat."

"Cut your throat! Who said anything about that? Look, when I was your age, I was a much better liar than you are right now. Do you want to know my secret?"

I remember feeling so relieved after learning I was not going to get my throat cut that day. All my life I was told lying was terrible, and now someone mentioned sometimes it was necessary. I got so confused. I agreed to learn about his secret, which had turned out to be our little secret.

I was still strapped in the chair as he put butter inside the homemade bread. I thought he was going to eat the bread himself, but it turned out it was my remedy. He freed me from the chair and handed me the home-made buttered bread and a glass of water. He told me to take a huge bite and gulp it down with some water. That way it would take the fish bone out of the way. I did what he instructed. It was excruciating at first, but I did feel relieved after I accomplished the mission. He ordered me to take another sip of water to make sure the annoying sensation was gone, but I was scared to do so. I was so relieved after he had healed me, I ran toward his front door to go back to the house to finish the rest of the food.

As soon as my right foot made it past the front door, Dave's father said to me, "I am guessing you do not need to know my secret anymore. At least you could've thanked me for not cutting your throat."

I rushed right back into his so-called office and sat on the same chair he strapped me in before. I thanked him for leaving my throat intact and begged him for minutes to tell me about his secrets. He started by saying not to abuse this secret; it was not funny to lie for nothing. Lie to defend oneself. Lie to protect your loved ones. He made me take an oath not to abuse his method and not to lie just because I could. The secret was plain and simple. He whispered in my ear because he did not want his wife or his older son to figure out he was teaching a six-year-old kid how to lie.

He leaned toward my left ear and said, "It is not that difficult. If you do not believe in your lie, nobody else will. Make the lie your truth; only then people will believe you."

That was easy to say but harder to do. Practice and persistence would later help me master this trick.

To master this trick, I had to violate the oath I had taken. Stevenson was the first one I had experimented that secret on, and to be honest, it was fun. I would tell him a bunch of fake stories about how I used to live in *Delmas* before I ended up in here with him. I would say to him I had lots of cars, and I used to live in a huge mansion with lots and lots of girls and mad friends. Sometimes, the stories did not make any sense at all, but me believing in such a fake story made Stevenson want to live the fake life I had before that one. Eventually, I had to tell him the truth; I had to say to him such a life never existed, and I made the whole thing up.

He looked at me and said, "You are just the master of lying, man, and I want you to teach me how to do this."

One of the best things I have accomplished in life is the fact I never taught him how to lie.

CHAPTER TEN

WELCOME TO PURGATORY

I used to literally look down on people. I loved that house we had back in Hell. Sitting on that balcony and look down on the others would make me feel like I was superior, and I would think I was more valuable than the others. In a way, I was more than an ignorant person; I was what you would call "A bleeding idiot" for thinking in such a way. My godfather's house would be one of many reasons why that type of reasoning ceased to exist. No upstairs balcony would allow me to classify myself as the better person, and the only *galeri* were there as soon as you open the second middle door. When you sat on that balcony, you could see the path to Hell and across from that balcony was Jean's older son's room, which would become his room when his son and wife left. That room was on the right side of a long hallway, similar to the one we had in my childhood home in Hell. Two more rooms would follow, another one on the right side, right next to his bedroom, this room was occupied by the mermaid's daughters and my godmother back then. The last bedroom was where the hallway ended, and the mermaid and my godfather settled on that one years ago. Nobody was allowed to enter this room without their approval.

The mermaid and Jean's bedroom would become Yaya's bedroom as we moved in. Stevenson and I had occupied the middle bedroom, which was utilized by the mermaid's daughters. My godfather seized the third one. He set it up real nice, and it sort of looked like a teenager's room with gun posters and soccer themed ones too. He would spend his whole day in this room, for he was very sick. Ever since we moved in, things changed, and my aunt was able to take better care of him. I did not know what he suffered from; we did not have that type of bond at the beginning. We usually talked whenever I had done something wrong or when he was giving me the "man talk." I knew his disease was severe because he had to go to Cuba to get his treatments, which had made Aunt Cleante a very sad, lonely, and at the same time delighted mother.

At the end of the hallway, you had to take a left to gain access to the dining room, and if you kept on walking straight, you ended up in a small storage room, and on the left of that storage room was the door that led to the kitchen. There was another door in the kitchen, and that was the one I left open when Bebi went away for the holidays. That door led to the backyard/garage, and when you exited that door, there was a small staircase, and on the right side of it, you would find a big reservoir. That was where we stored water for daily use. Walking down the backyard/garage, you could spot the big front gate, and on the left of it, you would meet with the staircase in front of the balcony and the *boutik*, which was empty at that time. We would use it to store cement and sell them, and later on we would sell kerosene by gallons in there as well. Past that *boutik* was the third door, the one that was never used.

There also was an outside hallway, and that one was wider than the one that was inside the house. That hallway started by the *boutik's* front wall and ended up by the wall that created the alleyway that led up to *Impasse Jean Thomas*. There was no bathroom, but on the left side of where the outside hallway ended, we used that space to take showers, and not too far from it was the latrine. That was the worst part of the house, and at times, it smelled. Because of that smell, I would spend days without taking dumps. That would be one of the reasons why we had to leave Purgatory for Heaven. The one thing I liked from that house was the fact I could gain access to the roof quickly and it was not as high as the one back in Hell. There was an almond tree in front of the staircase that was connected to the balcony. Stevenson and I would go up to the roof and pick the almonds straight from the tree. That was the easier way for us to get them. There were other ways of gaining access to the almonds. Most kids would throw rocks at them, but someone might get hurt like I did one day. Others used a stick with a bent metal at the end (*Gol*) to pull them from the tree.

I would use the roof to get away from distractions whenever I was studying for upcoming exams. That was the place I used to go to find peace. That was the place where I wrote my first poem. Purgatory had started to grow on me; I began to master the talent I never knew I possessed. Talented people surrounded me most of the times, and that was the reason behind the fact I found poetry. Behind the house, on the other street named *Impasse Jean Thomas*, was another house, and my English teacher lived there. Later on, another young guy would move in with him. This guy's name was Stevie, and he used to sell *Pappadap* in front of his house. *Pappadap* was a system used by a phone company in Haiti that allowed you to let other people use your house phone and get paid for the exact amount of time they used it. It was more like a payphone, except someone was watching you the whole time.

A lot of us would gather right next to him where he would be stationed to sell *Pappadap* to talk about everyday activities. We would crack jokes and also debate about political issues and hip-hop. These sorts of debate would later on be the cause of the birth of their rap group. There were five of them in the group, and they called it "RDR" which stood for "*Rassemblement Des Rappeurs,*" which means "*Rappers Gathering.*" I was not a member, but Stevenson's two best friends were members of the group. That was when my love for poetry had grown exponentially. I would listen to them freestyling, and I would record it then go home, sit on the roof, and analyze the song verse by verse. I would rewrite their lyrics and keep them to myself hoping they would buy the best version of their work from me. Unfortunately, that rap group did not even last a good six months. They went back to being cool fellows and kept on debating. In that same house where Stevie lived there was a great trumpet player. I never saw him, but the way he played the trumpet was in accord with my ears. I would sometimes wake up to the sound of his musical notes.

When you exited the front door, the middle one, on your left side would be the house that formed the alleyway with mine. My classmate resided in this house, and he was the neighborhood's only bodybuilder. I would call him Rambo because of the size of his traps, biceps, and chest. He was a walking tank, and he was not the guy you wanted to piss off. He was not the aggressive type—given the way he looked you'd think he was. If you messed with him he would probably try to calm the situation down. If that was not the case, then you would need a fast trip to the hospital. I was intimidated by him, and that was one of the reasons why I wanted to be like him. I wanted the boys in the neighborhood to fear me, and I wanted to be respected just like most people did him. Even his voice seemed to be lifting weights as well; he had a very aggressive tone. That was the type of sound that would make any weak man shit his pants. Even when we were cracking jokes, his laugh would be the meanest one I have ever heard, but he was a cool fellow, and I have enjoyed every single time I have spent with him.

When I was not home, you would find me in his house, chilling by playing cards or dominoes with his sisters and cousin. During exam week, I would spend the entire night studying with him, and sometimes those study nights would turn into fun nights where we would eat and play games on his computer. There was one game he loved to play, and it was a very difficult one. It was called "*Deshabille moi*," which is French for "undress me." Interesting game if you ask me, but a tough one to beat.

The point of the game was to take a model's clothes off by catching falling beer bottles with a beer crate. The model would be fully clothed on the right side of the screen, and the left side was where you needed to catch the beer bottles. Rambo was the only guy ever to take off the model's bra, and that day was just the best day of his life. I could tell how happy he was, for he hugged me as if he had won the lottery.

Rambo had two sisters and a cousin who was very close to me. We were so close Rambo's father thought we were engaging sexually, but at the time I knew nothing about women or sex. I believe it would take the second coming of Christ for me to even kiss a girl on the lips during this time. I was not the type to go after girls or to feel the need to have a girl-friend. Speaking of which, I did have one back in Hell. She was my first girlfriend and that was not the type of relationship ordinary people had. At that time, this was the best relationship ever. I would later realize the best relationship was the one you are not a part of, and the one I had with my first girlfriend would prove that. Jumel was Rambo's cousin's name, and she was a very stunning woman. She was caring, loving, and very respectful. That was the first best female friend I ever had, and she had opened my eyes to reality.

Now that I was a teenager, there were some things I could not tell Yaya, but with Jumel, I felt at ease telling her everything. She knew about my deepest secret and the wrongdoings I did to Stevenson. She would be the reason I changed my behavior and my ways against him. The abusing stopped, and I was glad it did because she made me realized how bad I would feel if I was in Stevenson's shoes. That was not a gift anybody possessed. You could say these things to anybody, but making them feel something they had been doing to another was a whole different thing. I remembered that night we were sitting on the roof of Rambo's house. That was when she was going to bring my true self out. It started pouring, and we made our way down to her bedroom. I was sitting on the floor, my back on the side of her bed, and she was lying on her stomach on the mattress and making eye contact with me through the mirror that was in front of us. She was a real one, and she was the first woman ever to make me feel sorry about the type of person I used to be. She was the first woman to make me feel guilty about the things I had done back in Hell.

◆　◆　◆

That night, I transitioned from "Jenkins the abuser" to "Jenkins the human." Jenkins the human being was born that night. After feeling bad about what I had done to Stevenson, I went straight to my house in hope to find Stevenson and apologize, but he was not there. He was with his two best friends hanging out at *Impasse Jean Thomas*. When he finally came home, I tried to apologize, but I realized he would forgive me, and to be honest, I did not deserve to be forgiven. I still don't deserve it.

When he came home all wet from the heavy rain, I asked him: "Where have you been? I have been looking for you, and I got something to tell you, man."

With his head down, he replied, "Oh, I was just hanging out with Fefe and Wendy, and I finally got to talk to that girl I like."

That was the first time in my life I felt so happy for him. Unlike me, he knew his way around women.

"What is it you wanted to tell me?" he asked me while he was enjoying the fact he was happy from talking to that girl.

At this point, I did not want to ruin such a good feeling he was having, I did not want to bother him by bringing up the messed up things I have done to him.

I just tapped him on the shoulder and said, "Nothing brother, I'm happy for you, and I hope you do earn that girl's heart."

"Earn her heart? Noooooooo, I want to earn her panties," he replied as he was rocking his body back and forth laughing.

We both laughed, not because I thought what he said was funny, but because all my life I realized even though I was traumatizing him he still managed to get past my terrors and find a way to be happy. That was something I would never be able to do, and I admired him for it. He was a real prick too, but a hilarious one. Despite everything, he would always stay by my side whatever the situation was, and he would never, ever rat me out. I was not much of a fighter, but he would fight my battles for me. Anybody who messed with me messed with him as well, but I was too dumb and too stupid to see that. This neighborhood opened my eyes to see that version of him I never knew existed. Most people would describe him as an old soul; he was just a super friendly kid and one you'd like to be around all the time. He was the spitting image of my godfather and us living under the same roof with his dad forced us to be on our best behavior. Stevenson and I used to spend most of our afternoons on the roof of the house, and that would be the place where he showed me how real of a prick he was.

It was probably four in the afternoon, and my godfather was in his room, resting. My aunt was sitting on the balcony listening to gospel music while she was praying. Stevenson and I, after finishing our dinner, decided to get up the roof and spend the rest of the day gazing over the neighborhood while playing cards. His two best friends joined us, but they did not stay for long because their aunt was a mean one. We checked the girls passing through the alleyway and sometimes tried to interact with them. I, on the other hand, was not too successful with this process. Stevenson would always get their attention, but when it came to me, they would ignore. There was one girl, she was also a member of Purgatory, and I did manage to get her attention.

As we were talking, Stevenson decided to interrupt our conversation by stating, "When did you start wearing glasses? They look good on you."

I had never seen a girl blush from such a simple sentence. Maybe there were more to it, but she did turn completely red given the fact she was light skinned.

In my mind, I was like, *How do you do that!* It was like watching a magician performing his best magic trick.

The girl's response was, "Thank you. You are such a cutie...I have been wearing glasses for a long time. I have trouble reading sometimes."

At this point, I was at war with myself. I thought to myself, *I was the one who approached you, why are you talking to him?* I did not want to say that out loud, and if I did, it'd make me look even worse than I already did.

Stevenson looked at me for a split second and whispered, "Just watch, it is about to go down." He turned back around and faced the girl then shouted, "Is that right, you cannot read without them? Maybe you are wearing them just to see the SIZE OF THE PENISES!"

That was the first time in my life where I witnessed someone going from being happy from a simple compliment to being very sad quickly. I could tell from the look on her face she regretted the fact she stopped to listen to such madness. That girl would, later on, hate me. I knew that was not fair, the fact she ended up being besties with Stevenson days later after such humiliation. I tried to apologize to her because I felt if I hadn't talked to her that day she would have never felt the way she did. That did not go so well, and it was ironic how she called me a prick. Stevenson, who was a bit younger than me, taught me something that, until this day, I found very hard to be true.

He would tell me: "Girls do not like romance. They do not want you to be nice to them. They like assholes like me. They are hoping they can change me into being good. That is what they are chasing."

I could not even process such a thing at that time. It did not make any sense to me.

He then proceeded by telling me, "You are too kind, too nice, and you do not need repair, so they do not want you. They want me because I am the one who needs fixing."

Purgatory was the place where I first had to deal with real loss. I had experienced losing people before when I was in Hell. Death was always around over there. In Purgatory, I had to deal with death taking the people who were close to me. Back in Hell, one of our neighbors had died; at that time I had no idea what death was. I used to think only the grown-ups knew what it was because they would be crying and most of the time passing out over the dead. I came to realize nobody truly knows what death is. The first family member I lost was my godfather, and frankly, I did not know how to act. I was the calmest person in the house while others were crying and yelling all day. I could not choose how to feel at that time, and if I had to, I would be acting like everyone else. Some would say death is not the end, it is another beginning. I would say death is a gift. It is the only thing in life that teaches us how to honor someone properly.

CHAPTER ELEVEN

PURGATORY'S GIFT

I do not remember the day of the week, but I do know I had an exam coming up. My godfather was in the hospital after he was having trouble sleeping. He went to Cuba and quickly came back. I remembered how happy his mother was as he lifted her in the air. I knew he did not have the surgery he was supposed to have over there, and that same night things started to shift for the worse. Someone had driven him to the hospital the next morning. Yaya had a feeling he was not going to make it, for he went blind that day. She mentioned around nine in the morning Stevenson woke him up so he could take his morning showers. Jean had told him it was still dark outside and let him sleep some more when the sun was shining. He ended up in the hospital that day, and the next day we got the bad news. I was the first to know he was gone. I used to get up early in the morning, around four, to get ready for exams. That way it is quiet enough, and my mind is sufficiently empty to store tremendous amounts of information.

As I sat on top of the Range Rover that was parked in the backyard, I saw two of his best friends coming in through the front gate. One of them was empty-handed, and the other had a clear handbag with my godfather's clothes inside of it and a pillow with a significant amount of blood on it.

"He is dead, isn't he?" I asked the guy holding the bloody headrest.

He could not speak; he was very emotional as tears were running down his cheeks. After realizing he was dead, I quickly got off the top of the Range Rover and made my way to my room where I laid flat on my stomach on my bed and pulled the blanket to cover my entire body. I had no idea why I had done that. Maybe I was in shock. Perhaps I could not believe such news, but one thing was sure, he was seriously gone. I had always found it unfair how death decided to take him away right when we were about to get along. Our relationship was not that great given the fact he was known for beating our asses, but a couple of weeks before he had passed, we had a bond. It was not a strong one, it was getting there, but we talked about the father-son topics.

Besides being the punisher, he was a pretty cool friend. He would not let us see that side of him because we would not have feared him enough. He needed to hide that part of himself from us to terrorize us better. He was a formidable fellow, obviously really good with women. I am guessing that is why Stevenson was good with them as well. Before he left us, he had shown me that part of him for two weeks. It was like he knew his time was going to expire, and he wanted me to know the real version of him, not just the aggressor, but the big brother, the best friend I'd ever had. It was like he was rebirthed; he became humble just like his mother. It was so real that at some point I thought he was messing with me.

The first of those two best weeks I had with him were just unbeliev-able. I never thought he paid much attention to me. That first week I had become his only son. That day, Yaya was not in the house. She went to church, and Stevenson was probably out with his best mates. It was nine in the morning, and Jean's mother was still at Ms. Virgine's house. It was just the two of us in the house, and it got sort of awkward for a long time. He was in his room as I sat on the rocking chair on the balcony, I would try not to make eye contact with him because every time I did, he would smile, and I thought it was sort of creepy. I thought of leaving the house at that point, but I did not want to leave him alone in case he needed help with something.

He then got up from his bed and walked up toward me and said, "Get up, I need to use the chair...and make sure you help me sit."

I was already up before he could finish his sentence. He reached into his pocket then told me to look away. He would ask me to turn back around and face him, then he'd give me fifteen dollars and ordered me to buy some mangoes and to keep the change.

I bought fifteen dollars worth of mangoes, and at that time, that would be around twenty to twenty-five big mangoes. I put them all in a bucket and carried them on my head to the house. When I got there he looked at me and started laughing hard.

"What were you thinking?" he said to me, "Are you going to resell those? I only needed three of them, not the whole bucket."

As I struggled to put the bucket to the floor, I said, "Well, you told me to keep the change. It was mine to do as I pleased, so I figure we could have a mango eating contest. Are you ready?"

At this point, I had done the impossible. I made my godfather laugh so hard I had to carry him to the restroom while he was crying laughing. When we came back, I settled him back on that rocking chair while he ordered me to get a small chair from the kitchen so I could sit beside him.

With the bucket of mangoes in the middle of us, we sat not too far from each other, and he yelled, "LET THE CONTEST BEGIN!"

It was not a real contest; we were having fun biting into the juiciest mangoes in Purgatory. He ate a mango by first making a *Totot* with it. *Totot* is when you take the mango, and you hit it against the wall repeatedly to make it soft. Then you have to bite a small hole on the bottom of the mango and start sucking its juice. I am not particularly eager to eat mangoes that way; I like them more when they are sliced, and that was my biggest challenge because I had no idea how to slice a mango properly at the time.

I sat there and watched him eat up his mangoes until he asked me, "Aren't you going to eat yours?"

I replied by saying: "Yes, but..."

He interrupted me by finishing my sentence for me by blurting out, "But you like them sliced. Go get a knife in the kitchen. I'll slice them for you."

I was not expecting that from him. I got up and stood there for a minute and took a good look at him as he was staring back at me. My thought at that moment was, *I should tell him I love him, but that would be too weird.*

As I was thinking, he said, "Do you need a picture? Go get the damn knife, kid."

"Yes, yes, knife...I am going to get it," I said back to him as I rushed to the kitchen.

I guess this was what he had to do for me to appreciate him. The slicing of some mangoes, that's all it took. I was not too hard to be pleased. I grabbed the knife and handed it over to him. Then he picked the biggest mango in the bucket and sliced it while he had one in his mouth.

He said, "Look closely at how I am slicing this mango. I won't be around forever to be slicing them for you."

I did look, and still to this day I cannot do it as he did. He must be very disappointed.

He handed me the last slice and then said, "It is your turn now. Show me what you've learned."

I took the knife from him while I was nervously laughing, picked a mango from the bucket, and started to slice the hell out of it.

When I was done with all the slicing, he looked at the mango and said, "I'd hate to be that mango right now, but not bad. You will get better."

We kept on eating mangoes until the bucket was empty and I told him, "You will get better. You will be just fine *parenn* (Godfather)."

He looked back at me with a mango seed in his left hand and said, "You don't know it, but you might've just added an extra day for me to survive."

After saying that, that same "I love you" feeling came back, and I wished I had said it to him.

The second week was even better. As a fifteen-year-old teenager, I am not ashamed to say I did not know how to shower properly, and he would tell me the secret about taking a perfect one. Whenever CAMEP decided to let us have access to running water, Stevenson, Jean, and I would use the hose and shower together. He'd put the pressure high to spray us so hard we would hit the floor or the wall. Those were the fun times, but the funniest part was when he taught us how to wash our body correctly. I would take the bar of soap and rub on my belly up until I got that foam and applied it to the rest of my body. He said no, that was not the right way to do that.

He asked me, "Do you know why God gave you pubic hair?"

I would awkwardly answer, "Noooo?"

He'd say, "He gave them to you so you could use it to create more foam by rubbing the soap on them, not on your belly."

To those words, I was astonished, I quickly took my soap bar and gently rubbed it underneath my wet underwear, and there it was, I had enough foam to wash the whole house.

He would continue by telling me I need to use a rag to scrub my body. I saw him using cloths before, but I always thought it was nasty to use the same rag over and over again. Whenever I was done taking showers, the water wouldn't stay still on my body like it did his. When he was showering, you could spot the water drops staying on his body like they were huge pimples. I never thought that was possible. On the other hand, whenever I took a shower it looked like I had wasted a whole bottle of lotion on my body. It would seem like I wasted a whole gallon of olive oil. Not only did I look shiny, if you were to run your finger on my body it would be very slippery. He gave me the secret to have the water droplets staying still on my body, a mystery that had been useful for a long time. Not only did I have to scrub my body, but I had to use the soap up until I could not run my fingers smoothly on my body.

Besides that, he would be the first person to let me get a hold of his guns. He was a businessman; he ran an essential business. His cousin, Daddy, had sent him a Mack truck he used to rent people who needed to transport materials for construction. He did not have a garage to park that truck; he had to park it outside of the house with the other cars he owned. To ensure his business, he had to get his gun license, and with it, he bought two guns. He referred to them as his *"two favorite dogs."* He was a dog person, and I was not surprised at all he named his guns after his favorite animal. He would use the gun only if he spotted people creeping around his cars, more importantly, that Mack truck. People would then steal the car's tires and come back in the morning and try to sell them back to him. He was a victim of that more than twice. That resulted in him getting the guns and scaring the thieves away. He would not shoot at them. He'd shoot in the air, and in the morning I would see bullet shell casing on the floor, and I would collect them and show them to my friends. That made me look cool for a while up until I got into real trouble with the school.

I was always looking for his "dogs," constantly looking through his stuff hoping to find them, but the search was never a success. I knew they were in the house, and I was too scared to ask him where he was hiding them. I already figured out he would not give me the secret spot. I would have done the same if I had kids around my house. I just wanted to hold them and perhaps take some pictures while posing as *Hitman* or *James Bond*. When he left for the hospital for his check-ups, I'd turn his room upside down to find the "dogs," but it seemed like the "dogs" did not want to be found. Stevenson would tell me to give up, and maybe they were not in the house, maybe he gave them to his older son. I would tell him I could sense them in the house. It was like I was living in a haunted house, except the "dogs" were the ghosts. They would call out my name, haunt me at night, even keep me up all night playing that unfair hide and seek game.

Back in the days when I was probably seven years of age, I'd spot him showing them to the guys working on his truck. I remember one of his vehicles had an engine problem, and he had asked a couple a mechanics to come to Purgatory to replace it for him. They would show up, set their working stations in front of the house, and set a pulley to lift the old engine out and install the new one. That type of work almost took them the whole day, and I remember standing there the entire day watching their every single move. I remember being chased by him a couple of times because I was messing with the mechanics' tools, but I just wanted to be around and be helpful to them. I spent most of my time dealing with women, and I remember feeling the need to help those mechanics in any way I could. One of the mechanics, the coolest one, was very understanding. He told my godfather it was okay for me to keep them company. He asked me for the tools he needed to use, and I would hand them to him. They started talking about how business was going, and before I know it, my godfather went into his room and brought out a silver box with a black handle.

He opened the box then said, "This is all the protection one needs, guys."

I desperately wanted to get a hold of them, but I was so scared of him, I did not even bother to ask. I just kept on waiting to hand over the next tool that was needed.

I caught a glimpse of them. One of them was silver because the sun's rays bouncing off that gun was trying to make me go blind, and the other one was black. He'd take the mags off of them and let the mechanics hold them for a minute; they were in awe. That was the first time I saw his "dogs." The second time I saw them would be amazing. Not only did I get to see them, but I would have the chance to hold them as well. Not too long after he had shown me how to shower properly, he showed me where he had the guns hidden, and I felt so stupid for not finding out. He hid them in plain sight. We were both sitting on the balcony that day talking about school and everyday type of things, and suddenly it got very boring. He had told me I could go outside and have fun with the other kids, but I wanted to stay with him because we had an unbreakable bond now, and I wanted us to be tighter than we ever were. I kindly rejected his offer and told him I was fine right where I was.

Suddenly he got up and said, "I got something to show you. Follow me, kid."

I followed him to my room, and as soon as you entered my room, on the left side was a wardrobe. Nobody used it because it was not good. We left it there so we could use the mirror that was on its door. He then got on his knees and opened a small door on the base of that wardrobe, and there it was, that same silver box I had seen nine years ago. I should have known that was where he hid them because that was the same place he used to keep the bullets, on the top of that wardrobe.

He held the guns by their barrels and took off the clips. He did some other stuff to the gun that I had no idea of, then he handed them to me. I was scared to take them, but at the same time, I could not believe that was happening. My godfather gave me his guns, and at that time I remembered thinking maybe he was going crazy. I thought that because I remembered he whooped my ass over a toy gun a long time ago, and now he was handing me real ones; something was not right with that picture. My mind raced back in time as I tried to remember how he whooped me with this belt, and at the same time, my heart was pounding, ready to leave my chest and meet the gun before my hands had the chance to meet them first.

"I'm handing you my dogs, kid. I know you have been looking for them. Here they are. Take them, make your dream come true," he said to me with a straight face and a weird smile.

I did not know if I could trust him. I thought maybe that was a trap. Maybe he was testing me, but I desperately wanted to go for them.

As he was going to put the "dogs" back in their cages, I held his strong left hand that was holding the silver one and said, "Wait a minute, aren't you going to be mad?"

"Mad?"

"Mad at me for holding the guns."

"You mean mad at you for holding the guns I asked you if you wanted to hold?"

"Yeah?"

"No, I am not going to be mad, kid. Here, just take the damn dogs."

I took the "dogs" from him.

I loved that side of my godfather. For someone who was raised without a father around, those two weeks I had to spend with my godfather taught me I had one, I was just too dumb to realize that. He was too busy focusing on straightening me out, he forgot to show me the best version of himself. My small and very skinny arm could not keep up with the weight of the "dogs." As soon as he gave them to me, their loads almost pulled me to the floor. I could not believe I was holding guns. Now I wanted to do more. I wanted to go outside and show them to the kids in the neighborhoods. I remembered feeling the need to take them to school and wear them across my belt to scare off that guy who used to bully the heck out of me. For a moment, I felt like I was on top of the world, and my godfather looked at me as if he was proud of me getting my hands on his guns. I pointed them on my bed and made dumb gun sounds, and Jean laughed and called me stupid names. That day was too good to be true. This was the last memory I wanted to leave my mind during my last day on this planet.

CHAPTER TWELVE

MY MOST GIFTED DAY

As I laid there on my bed, face down to the pillow under a huge blanket that covered my entire body, I could sense Yaya had heard the bad news. In Haiti, it was hard not to notice someone had died in your neighborhood. The cries and the banner the private morgue would put on your wall or door were signs of that. You had to be blind and deaf not to notice death had visited someone. The neighborhood had a different vibe, especially if that person was well known like my godfather. The whole community was pretty quiet. That was the first time I had heard my aunt cry. It was not pleasant because I remembered having that urge to cry as well, but for some reason, I felt like that day I had no tears left in me. I did not know how to handle or how to act in this situation; all I was doing was being calm under that blanket for about fifteen minutes. During those fifteen minutes, my aunt tried to get me to come outside, but I was not feeling it, I did not want to be the odd one out there. I did not want to be out there looking all calm while all the other people in the neighborhood were sad and crying as if one of their family members had died.

Before I knew it, the house was filled with people. People came from different neighborhoods, even people from the countryside traveled miles to come and support us during that time. That blanket was like a time machine for me. While I was under there, I could relive all the fun times I have had with him. It was not like I could not believe the fact he was gone. I had made my peace with the fact someday I would not be surrounded by the people I admired the most. It was more like it happened too soon, and I was not expecting him to leave that early. That had me thinking maybe he had gone a day later because he told me I might have added an extra day to the ones that were assigned to him just because I said to him he would be fine. Maybe I did, perhaps I did not, but up until this day, I am still wondering if I lied to him or if I assured him he would be able to make it past the day he was supposed to go.

At some point during the day, I had to get out of my room; I had to get ready to take that test. I was about to be tested on my least favorite course. I was not too fond of it. It was French literature, and whenever the professor was teaching, my mind was somewhere else, I could not focus one bit on what he was saying. I had to come up with a plan to escape my room to get ready for the exam. While I was in there, I stood in front of the mirror practicing the best sad face I thought would be perfect to blend in with everyone else. That was not successful, so finally, I decided to walk past them as calmly as possible. I opened the door and made my way through the hallway and ended up in the balcony where my aunt was sitting on the rocking chair, rocking back and forth with an old lady rubbing on her shoulder while she was crying. She looked at me, and suddenly I could see her pain, but I could not share her emotions, I could not join her. I do not know what it was about me that day, but I did not know how to be sad whenever someone had passed. Maybe I did, but I could not show it. It was the same thing with appreciation, I would appreciate someone for doing something for me, but it would not show.

After standing in the balcony witnessing my aunt being sad for the first time, seeing her crying for the first time, I made my way past the most sorrowful crowd ever and went to the back to take my morning shower. I could hear people asking who I was and why I was acting like everything was okay. I kept my cool and kept on going even though some of them might have thought I had no heart or no soul. Stevenson, on the other hand, was one of the saddest ones. I avoided talking to him that day because I wanted him to deal with his loss the best way he could. I did not want to upset him more than he already was. After taking the longest shower ever, I made my way past the saddest crowd again, except that time the crowd grew larger. People were blocking the front door as I was trying to get out and head to school.

As I was walking to school, part of me said maybe I should have stayed and grieved with all the others, but the other part was saying what good would that do? I made it to the school, but I was a bit early, so I stayed outside of the gates and talked to the other students who were also early. We had regular conversations, and we sort of reviewed for the test. To me, it was just another day. I did everything the same way I used to on the other days, but deep down I knew I had lost something, but I was struggling to show it. I thought of it as a curse. I felt I was cursed. I would cry for the wrong reasons, I would cry over idiotic things, but when it came to the guy who had shown me the best two weeks of my life, I could not shed a single tear. Before I knew it, the bell rang and it was time for us to head to our classroom and start taking the exam. I sat on my desk and I was given the paper containing around thirteen questions with half of them being essays. I would not say I liked essays, but for some reason I got them done. As always, I was the first student to leave the classroom, I was always the first to finish the other exams as well, and that meant I got to go home early. I did not want to go back to the mournful house, so I stayed around for a bit waiting for the other students to finish their tests so we could compare answers and make sure we had everything right.

The whole day, his death was occupying my mind; I could not stop thinking about it. I did not want to share it with my classmates, for I thought it was a personal matter, but talking to someone about it might have helped in a way. I tried to speak to Jumel about it, but she went to her mother's and would not come back until the next month. It was, in a way, sort of tough because I had no one to talk to about it. I had people around, but I wanted them to grieve properly. I did not want to interfere with their emotions. I was one of the last students to leave school, and when I did, I saw my French literature professor, and he had told me for the first time I had aced my exam. He did not give me the grade, but he used to look over the not-so-bright students' test first before he got to the real ones, and that way he would not have to worry about that when he got home. That day I had surprised him. He even thought I cheated somehow. How could I? I was sitting right in front of him.

By the time I got home, it was probably five o'clock. The house was not as packed as it was before, and it was pretty quiet. My aunt sat on the balcony accompanied by aunt Cleante, listening to gospel music and humming them at the same time. I kissed her on her right cheek and hugged my aunt and did not even bother to ask how they were doing. I figured that would be dumb considering how the situation was this morning when I left. I already knew the amount of pain they were enduring. Aunt Cleante's pain was probably the worst, losing the only son she loved so much, who must have taken some part of her away with him. She was not the same after his death, but she managed to be understanding, to be as calm as possible. She defended me while my aunt questioned my ability to be so quiet. She described it as if I did not even care my godfather had passed. Yaya also asked me not to use the TV, or even worse, not to play any video games considering the situation, but Aunt Cleante suggested otherwise. She told Yaya I could not choose how to feel about such a tragic moment, and I was too young to understand what was happening. That was probably the second time I let Aunt Yaya down. I could see the disappointment in her eyes as I headed to my room to spend the rest of the day in there.

Stevenson was out for the whole day. I had no idea how he took the news, but before I left for the exam, I could sense the sadness in him. It was dancing in his eyes. My best bet was he was hanging out with his best mates next door, talking to them hoping to feel a bit better. I understood why Stevenson would not speak to me, and I wanted him to, for I needed someone to talk to as well. I was not a good brother to him, and it was only fair he sought help elsewhere. He did come back late that night, and I had stayed up to see him. He looked tired. He was not the same energetic type of kid I knew. He was disconsolate, and his eyes were like a balloon filled with water and ready to burst at any moment. As he entered the room, I got up, and he paid no attention to me as he carelessly fell into his bed.

I told him to get up, but he refused my offer while holding his pillow to his face by saying, "Not now, man. Let me try to sleep."

I insisted, and he finally got up. I remembered how glad I felt that night when he finally agreed to get up.

I hugged him.

For the first time, I had hugged him, and it felt awesome. All the feelings that were building up inside of him came out that night as he cried his heart out. I had never been in this situation before where I had to try my best to comfort someone and try to stop the crying. While he was in my arms, I was thinking about that sign I saw at my school that read, "*A true friend is not the one who wipes the tears, it is the one who kept them from coming out.*"

From that moment, I realized I was not that true friend. I was just a friend, not a fake one, but one who knows when the other friend is in peril. It was the longest hug I have ever given anybody, and when I finally let go of him, he wiped his eyes dry and thanked me. Through the night we talked about everything except for the harsh moments I put him through. We talked about the fun memories we had with his dad and how he had turned our life around. Just like his grandmother, Cleante, he understood why I was not acting like everyone else. He would first tell me I was a weird one, and everyone grieved differently.

We talked our way to sleep, and in the middle of the night, when we had access to electricity, I woke him up and said, "Let's get lost in the Nintendo 64 world."

We've spent the whole night playing Mario Kart 64 up until Aunt Yaya showed up. I thought we were going to be in trouble because she did not want me to play earlier, but instead she offered us some of the chicken sandwiches she was about to make.

We both looked at each other and smiled, then looked back at my aunt with the same creepy smile while nodding our head affirmatively and said, "Yes, please. Thank you."

◆　◆　◆

My godfather's death was the preparation of an upcoming event, something I was meant to survive, a challenge I was destined to face. Such challenge was the last touch my soul needed to become entirely pure. For some people, it might require a little bit of work, but for me, it had to be that tragic event. Purgatory was not enough for me to find my true self; it was preparing me so I could be strong enough, good enough to enter Heaven and meet my better self. His death had made my dream come true, at least half of it. I have always dreamed, still dreaming one day I would be able to be around my whole family. All my life, I had only known two of my aunts, my grandmother, and one cousin, but I also wanted to see the ones who were living overseas, my other aunts, cousins, and uncles. I wanted to know where I came from; I wanted to know my whole family, and his death had made that possible.

The next day after his passing, we had some visitors. Family members from different places had come to our house for his wake. I do not do well around strangers. I was hiding in my room and tried to stay out of sight as they made their way inside. At some point, while I was hiding from them, I figured out I would not be able to hide forever. I would have to show myself. I could hear their voices making their way through the hallway, and they did not sound too happy. You could sense the sadness in them, and soon after the talking, the crying would follow. It was almost like the first day, but this time it was family only and a bit quiet. Part of me wanted to head out and meet them, but I was too shy and did not know how to greet or act around them. That was always an issue with me, and I tended to make things more awkward than they needed to be.

A few minutes had passed when one of my aunts from overseas asked about my whereabouts. I prayed Yaya would say she did not know, but she yelled out my name. I felt like I was compelled to come to her as she called, so I did. As I made my way through the hallway and ended up on the balcony where the strange faces were pointing directly at me, I felt paralyzed. I could not move a muscle, and only my eyes were moving left and right as they were scanning the new faces. The first person I noticed was my godfather's sister. She was pretty calm, just like her mother, but that would change during the funeral. I remember she brought a turkey with her, which my aunt had cooked for us. We sat together, and we ate while sharing the sweetest memories that he created with us before he passed. The whole time I stayed quiet. I did not want to share my memories. For some reason I thought once I shared them they would be out in the open for anyone else to take.

I stayed silent as his sister asked Yaya, "Is he always that quiet?"

I tried not to make any eye contact with anybody in the room when Yaya answered, "No, he is not always like that. You know, we have our way of dealing with losses. That's his way." They continued to talk, and everybody talked about how I was the spitting image of my mother. They would also refer to me as "*Ti Mireille.*" I learned much about my godfather that day, and I knew he was a troublemaker and if any of his kids had been like he was as a kid, he would have killed them. Like me, he used to cry a lot, and he was also a great soccer player. He had played for a soccer team in Haiti called "*Aigle Noir*" meaning "Black Eagle." That was the first official family meeting I ever had, and it was awesome. They asked me many questions, most of them about school and what I wanted to be. I answered them, but believe me when I say it was very awkward.

His passing made me think about death on a whole new level. Unlike everybody else, I did not consider death to be something terrible. I found death to be a gift, a way of recognizing what the loved one had done for us and all the trouble they kept us from getting into. It was only during a funeral or a wake people always talked about how good the deceased was and the good things they had done. Only then they appreciated what that person had done for them. We might have shown it to them when they are still alive, but not enough. I did not praise my godfather like I did while he was lying in that casket, so therefore death was a gift, a way of spitting out praises and appreciations to the deceased. It was not until then I realized how much he had done for me, and that taught me to appreciate people even more while they are still alive.

We had a little family wake; no friends were invited, no strangers. The reason behind that was because in Haiti whenever there was a wake (*Vey*) and anybody was welcome it tended to lead to chaos. People would fight; they would drink their asses off and start cussing throughout the night. They would sing songs filled with profanities and even have some cursing tournament, the one to have the meanest cuss would be the winner. They would make up songs as well and tried to lighten up sad people. That was the whole point of a *Vey* in Haiti. It was to make the deceased's family feel a bit better before the big day. That was not the case for us, although we did have a good time. We had told some jokes, learned a bit about the family, and we shared some more memories. I still did not share the ones I had with him. We then ate and ended up saying a prayer, and then we called it a night. The next day would be different. That day would be sadder than the first one when we had received the bad news.

It was a very short night. Before I could close my eyes to go to sleep, it was already morning, and it was time for me to get ready for the funeral. It was a quiet morning. I could hear the roosters crowing and the birds singing as the sun was rising above the horizon. I could smell the sweet aroma of coffee being brewed from Dave's house, which was how they started their mornings—with fresh brewed coffee and bread painted with local peanut butter. The smell of scrambled eggs swam around the house as my aunt fixed me a plate. Yaya and I were the first ones to get up that day, and the others were still sleeping. Some of them were having their half an hour prayer. Although my plate was already fixed, I did not start eating up until everybody else was up and feasting as well. While I was waiting for them to get up we were provided with electricity, so I took advantage of that by ironing my long-sleeved white shirt and the long, slim-fit black pants. The vest was good already, it did not need ironing, but I did it as well to kill time.

Before I knew it, everyone else was up and super quiet. The same sad faces from before came back, and Yaya was just not herself that day. She would not talk to anybody, and from time to time tears would come dripping down her cheeks. The funeral was set to take place around eleven in the morning, but we managed to be at the church precisely at that time. We all sat at the table to eat breakfast, and it was the most awkward breakfast I ever had. It was as quiet as a cemetery, and tears were served instead of juice. I wanted to break the silence, but I did not want to say something stupid. I was the type of kid who would yell out, "Is anybody ready for the funeral?"

That would set the table on fire if I let those words out of my mouth. I joined in and kept my mouth shut. I could not ask them how they were doing, for it was very obvious, and I felt like by asking that I would not get a delightful answer.

Not too soon after such an awkward breakfast, we got ready to hit the road. My aunt was wearing all white with a black hat, and I was wearing my long-sleeved white shirt with the vest and the long, slim-fit pants and black dress shoes. We were all ready to get going, but before we left, I believe the sister was having trouble with her shoes, and that was when she let out all her feelings. She started yelling and crying as Yaya hugged her and consoled her. You could see she was not ready to face such a big day. Nobody was, but I think I was more prepared than anybody else, and that made me feel a bit evil. Stevenson was wearing the same outfit as me, and he was very calm that day, and so was his grandmother, Cleante. The time had come for us to exit the house, and all eyes were on us as we were getting inside Jean's older son's car. We had to rent about five school buses for all the friends he had and people he had helped during his mission on earth. Most people knew him as "*Gwo Jean*" which means "Big Jean."

By the time we got to the church where the funeral had taken place, it was already eleven o' clock. The officials let all the family members enter the church first and take a look at the deceased lying there in the coffin. He looked like he was at peace. His beard was well lined up, and his hair well-cut too. He was well-dressed, and he had his hands crossed on top of his stomach. As I stood there in front of him while having my right arm around Stevenson's neck, reality kicked in. I started to realize all the things he had done for me. Back when I was living in Hell, I did not see him as a father figure. I did not even see him as a human being. I saw him as a brute. He was only present when it was time for me to get my ass whooped. As I was standing there, I realized I could have been among the kids who had been shot dead for stealing. I could have been one of the kids who had lost their lives by setting their parents' house on fire when they were playing with matches. Thanks to him, he had taught me to not participate in such activities. He was my hero, and before Jean had left us he made sure he was my best friend as well.

The service went well, and it was one of the saddest funerals I have ever attended. It was packed, and most people were crying and yelling. They even kept the priest from finishing the service. By the time we were done, we had to head for *La Plaine*, the place he was buried. It was a long drive from the city, and I guess that was where he wanted to rest eternally. I believed he chose that location not only because he liked it, but because that was where he had his first son. I had to get inside one of the school buses just so a friend of his could get in the family car, a very close friend. Stevenson and I got on the bus, and it was a bit fun. People were singing and telling riddles, and they were also sharing the experiences they had with him. There would be some crying on the bus, but it was not the way it was at the church.

When we got to *La Plaine*, we all got out of the school buses and headed to the house with a huge backyard where they had a private cemetery for family members only. As we got out of the school bus, we walked to the hearse in hope to help the other guys carrying the coffin. Unfortunately, they had enough guys, and we just had to follow them to the grave. When we got there, a construction worker was standing next to his open grave with a fair amount of bricks next to him and some fresh concrete he had made. He would use those to seal shut the tomb after they put my godfather inside of it. When the guys got next to his grave, they slid the coffin inside and waited for everybody, family and friends, to take turns throwing dirt on the coffin while it was inside the tomb. I did not want to do that; I thought it was very disrespectful, and I knew my godfather would not want anybody to put dirt on his well-polished coffin. When it was my turn to do so, I stopped and took a look at Yaya. She nodded positively, and that was my green light to proceed with the dirt throwing. It turned out it was a sign of paying respect to the dead, so I was told. In my mind, I knew Jean knew I had enough respect for him already, so what I just did did not matter. I was the last one to throw the dirt in there. I threw a small amount, small enough not to be noticeable. After I had done that, the construction worker used his tools and started sealing up the grave. As he laid down the last brick, everybody howled and sang a good-bye song.

Yaya came up to me and said, "It is all over now; let us head home."

The ride back home was satisfying. It was not as sad as driving to the church for the service. It was more like everyone had finally realized my godfather was gone for good, and they had made their peace with that. They had finally accepted the fact he was gone. That was pretty apparent to me the very first day, and that was when I realized how difficult death could be to some people even though they did not understand it. I could not react to something I did not understand. I guess I was created to be like that. I was not strong like some people would say. I did not take the news better than anyone else; I was just ignorant in a sense. I just had no idea of what was happening. Death is not something you can practice. You cannot have a feeling of what it is; therefore, I could not react to any-body who had passed at that time. People tried to tell me it was the fact you would never be able to see that person ever in your life, but the most precious thing we tend to forget are the memories. They are the only things guaranteed to stay. Anything else vanishes. That was how it worked for me; his good memories kept him alive in me. He made sure I had a great time with him, and those memories, nothing could ever take them away from my mind. Sometimes I think to myself maybe I could have spiced up those memories just a bit by telling him I loved him. The whole ride back I thought about it. I thought about it so hard I ended up having a dream about it.

In that dream, I told him I loved him.

A few months after the funeral, about six months later, I learned about shooting stars. In Haiti, whenever you saw a shooting star, that meant a soul had departed. That meant someone somewhere had passed. I learned from the guys who used to debate every night outside the house inside an abandoned car. Everything seemed to be back to normal after the funeral. People got back to their daily activities, Yaya got her smile back, and Cleante left for the states and never set foot in Haiti ever again. That was understandable, and I would probably do worse if I were in her situation. Before she left, I remember that day Stevenson and I were sitting on the balcony where she was soaking her feet in hot water containing some leaves. Someone told her this was good because of how shocked she was when she heard the news. We were all sitting there on the balcony, and the level of boredom was off the chart. She could sense we were bored, she then called her grandson, told him to dry up her feet then gave him some money so we could buy a soccer ball. We both went to the carrefour's market (*Mache Kafou*) to get the ball, and when we came back she was long gone. What we did not know was not too long after she left us, we would be witnesses to a shooting star.

CHAPTER THIRTEEN

DÉPART DU CRÉATEUR

"**O**h my God! did you see it? Please tell me you saw it; I cannot be the only one who saw that."

"See what? What are you talking about?" I said to Stevenson.

"The shooting star. It was a very bright one, You could not have missed that," he replied.

"Oh no, I saw it, and it is not a shooting star. It is some meteoroid falling into the planet's atmosphere. It is just a rock burning up. That is what you saw."

"Whatever you say, Mr. Science man. Well, it was beautiful," Stevenson said histerically.

"Beautiful? How is it that beautiful? Is someone dying a beautiful thing?"

"What does that have to do with the shooting star?"

"Stevenson! How can you not remember the fact that whenever you see a 'shooting star,' someone had passed?"

"Oh, that. I did not forget, and the sight is beautiful, not the meaning behind it, but did you see it?"

"Yes Stevenson, I did see it, and I wish I did not...."

After I finished conversing with Stevenson about the shooting star, I got up from the mat we were lying down upon while gazing at the night sky on the roof and made my way downstairs to meet with my bed. It was not up until the next day I had realized I had a reason for saying I wished I did not see that shooting star. I only said that because I wanted Stevenson to stop talking, given the fact he liked to talk a lot. He was going to spend the entire night talking about it and asking me questions about space stuff. The next morning would be one of the mornings that got me a head start about what was to come in Heaven. I remembered that night I had to study for a test I had to take the next day, a math exam. I wanted to prepare that night so I did not have to get up early in the morning. I figured I'd rather have a good night's sleep, then study in the morning when my mind is fresh. Something about studying under a kerosene lamp got me going about memorizing things. Most of the time I studied late at night when everybody else was sleeping. I did not prepare for the exam that night. I went straight to bed, and I fell asleep listening to Stevenson telling me some crazy bedtime stories he made up.

I slept soundly that night up until one in the morning when the alarm on my phone went off. It was studying time, and I did not want to wake Stevenson up, for he was going to distract me. It was still dark outside, and I had to light the kerosene lamp that was on the dining room table and settle there to start preparing for the test. It was pretty quiet, and you could still spot the stars in the sky. I could hear the leaves from the almond tree shaking due to the cold breeze passing through them, and I could also smell the fresh scent of the soil, for it was raining a little bit earlier before I got up. I sat on the table for about ten minutes, and then I heard someone yelling. At that moment, I realized I had heard that type of cry before. It was the cry of evil, the roar of death; this was the type of scream that would alert you someone had traveled to the other world. It was the type of cry that would pierce your soul and leave it injured for years to come. Besides the fact that the scream was the type you only heard when someone had died, something else made it sounds familiar as well.

The cry grew louder as the person who was screaming got closer and closer to the house. When I heard it clearly, I quickly put my pen down and made my way down the hallway hoping to find out what was going on. In Haiti, whenever you hear a weird sound or a cry, you best stay inside or something terrible might happen to you. We are very superstitious people, and at this time of the day, you should stay indoors to keep away from trouble. When I ended up on the balcony, I pulled up the shade just a little bit, enough for me to see what was going on outside. I scanned the dark street as my mind tried to process this familiar cry, and finally it hit me. It was the same cry I heard years ago when I was living in Hell. It was the same type of scream I heard when my cousin's best friend had passed. From realizing it was my cousin's, a cold breeze spread from my head down to my heels. I felt paralyzed after such a feeling; I knew something was wrong.

I did not know someone had passed up until she was banging on the door like a mad woman trying to let my aunt know about what happened. She was in shock, and she was upset, but I still had no idea what was going on. I might have had a clue, given the fact this was the only way someone had to cry when someone they love passed. Given the fact this cry was the same one my cousin let out when her best friend had passed, that helped me figure out how my day would go. I did not want to deal with another loss. I was not ready to go through what I went through with my godfather. I could not bear watching my aunt going through the same pain again, and that was going to be a challenge for me. I was not ready at all. I remember thinking I would have to find a way to blend in now since people were going to treat me as someone with no soul. My cousin kept on banging on the front door, and I did not go outside to let her in. I did not want to accept whatever she had to offer that day. I was still peeping through the shade when the knockings woke my aunt up. She made her way to the balcony to see what the case was as I was still trying to make sense of the situation.

"What are you doing here? Why aren't you opening the door for your cousin?" Yaya yelled at me as I made my way back to the dining room to finish preparing for the math exam. I could tell something was wrong. I could sense someone had passed given the fact Yaya had that same look on her face when she had learned my godfather had passed. As I sat on the dining table trying to focus on the preparation for the test, my aunt unlocked the door to let my cousin inside. I was trying my best not to let anything interfere with my study. When I studied for a test, I usually made up a test a month in advance and took it the day I was supposed to take the real one. Fifteen out of the twenty questions usually came out on the real one. That was my way of getting ready for whatever test it was, and my grandma Ana taught me that. She would examine how I was struggling in trying to memorize everything, so she would suggest I make an exam then take it over and over again based on what was taught in school during the semester.

Stevenson did not seem to be bothered by the crying because he was a heavy sleeper; you'd have to slap him endlessly to wake him up. When he finally got up, he usually blurted out some random words. The most common word Stevenson would spit out would be "*Sevyet*," which means "towel." I have tried to find out the reason behind why he does that every time we wake him up, but he does not remember saying any of that. That would remain a mystery never to be solved. A few minutes passed when my aunt joined my cousin, and now they were both crying. I got up from the table, dropped the books, and headed outside because when Yaya cried nothing else mattered to me but to make her feel a bit better. I saw both of them hugging while weeping and yelling. They ended up waking up the whole neighborhood. By then, it was obvious to me someone had passed, but I still did not know who it was. Part of me did not want to know, and I was hoping it was not a family member again because I did not want to put on the mask. I did not want to put on the veil that would make me feel and look like everybody else. I did not want to be judged as well, so it was obvious to me that day I would have to find a way to blend in.

At that time, I had seen a pattern. Every time I had an exam, a final exam, someone passed. I started to feel like I was death itself. I began to blame myself for all these deaths that were happening around me, and that would be the cause of associating myself to "Death" in that little rap group we had formed. It was the three of us, my best friend, Stevenson, and I. We would freestyle every night in front of the house, and Dave would be the judge. They did not write anything. I did most of the writings because it was kind of tough for me to come up with a good line out of the blue. I would write my verses, and Stevenson and my best friend would go from the top of their heads. They would think I called myself "Death" just because I wanted to be feared, but the truth was I wanted to take death's place so I could stay away from my family. I named myself like that so I could stay away from the ones who resided deep within my heart.

I did not know how to act in this situation, so I decided to sit on the back of a car that was parked outside for about twenty minutes by myself. I headed back inside to finish up with the studies. I was sort of tired of watching such sadness dancing in the neighborhood that early. The news was not private anymore. Everybody else was aware of what was going on, but nobody knew who had passed. As I was making my way back to my books, Yaya pulled me over, and I landed between her comfortable arms. That was the first time she had hugged me that hard, and I could feel her pain as her tears washed the back of my T-shirt. I put my arms around her and rocked her side to side in hope it would stop her from crying, but that was not successful.

That seemed to upset her even more, and she kept on saying: "She had passed without taking Christ as her savior. She did not even give me the chance to tell her I was sorry...."

That was the hint I was looking for, and right then and there I knew who had passed. I was hoping it was one of my cousin's friends again because I had seen what my godfather's death had done to my aunt. I did not think she was ready to lose anybody else in the family.

I did not want it to be true, but I also knew it was going to happen someday, but not that soon.

After Yaya blurted out those words, I held her by her shoulders and looked right in her eyes and nodded while I kept on saying, "No, no, no...."

She then nodded back affirmatively as I let go of her and headed back to my room and pulled the blanket over my head. Stevenson was still sleeping, snoring with his mouth wide open as he whistled when he exhaled. While I was under that blanket, I did not go back in time just like I did when Jean had passed. I stayed under there and tried to figure out why did it have to be that way? Why do we always have to deal with such sadness and wounds that take years to heal properly? I also thought this loss was my ticket back to Hell, not that I had not been back there since we have moved to Purgatory, but that would be one of the most important trips to Hell I'd have to take.

I had been back to Hell more than I could count. That was where I was forged, that was the neighborhood that showed me how much of a prick I was. That was also the neighborhood where I first saw the woman who made me do the impossible, the woman who allowed me to live while my heart stopped beating. How could I forget Hell? Hell was, still is, and always will be home. That was where my soul had been installed into my body, that was where my mind belonged. I had been over there plenty of times, but I never set foot in the house, not because I did not want to, but because it seemed like the house had lost its value. The house lost its soul, and it did not feel the same as when Yaya was part of it. Every time I knocked on the door, no one answered. It was always empty because it was only occupied by my cousin at that time, and most of the times she was not there. She was either in school or out with her friends. Besides that, whenever my grandmother came to Haiti, she never resided in that house ever since we moved. She used to stay at her worshiping lodge. She built a second story where she had everything she needed; there was no need for me to go back to that house now. Everything that made that house great was gone. Whenever I go back there, I would go straight to the soccer field, and right next to it was my first love's house.

Sometimes I would be the very first person sitting on that field. I would sit there even if I did not have a ball to kick around. I'd sit there to think while I was gazing at the house that used to be "Paradise in Hell." Most of the time, there would be people playing board games, most of them grown men, and I would stand there to watch and learn their every move. If that were not the case, then I would go to one of my friends' houses and sit on the roof and enjoy the beautiful sun. Around noon, everybody would be out either playing soccer or joking around. Since I was terrible at playing soccer, I would be the goalie and try to save as many painful shots as I possibly could. This field was the place where I could find contentment, and this was the place that set my mind right and gave me a reason to keep on pushing. That was where you would see me when things got tough. That field was my second home in Hell.

Before I knew it, it was already time for me to go back to that house, the house in which I had spent my entire childhood. That day, it was not as sad as Jean's passing because the deceased was not from Purgatory, she was not well-known in this community. There were not many strangers yelling and crying. It was just my aunt and Stevenson, but you could still sense the sadness around. Stevenson did not seem surprised when he heard the news, and I thought he got used to the fact people would always be leaving. It was tough for him when his dad had passed, and I thought maybe this one would not hurt him as much. That morning was somewhat similar to the one when Jean had passed. I did the same thing; I got ready to take the exam. This time it was different. I hugged my aunt and told her I'd be back as soon as I was done with the test. To me, it was just another day, but I still could not get my mind around the fact death was a part of me, I felt so responsible for losing such role models in my life. Besides that, I aced that math test just like that literature one, and I got out before anyone else. I did not stay around and talk to my classmates about the test. I just left in a hurry. I ran all the way home hoping to find Yaya, but when I got there she was not in the house. Stevenson had no idea of her whereabouts. With my uniform still on, I ran as fast as I could to Hell to see if she was with my cousin given the fact she was crying so much that morning.

When I got there, all eyes were on me. The ones who had not seen me around kept asking me questions about how I was doing and how things were going. They told me how tall I got and how I still had that creepy smile they seemed to enjoy. After spending about ten to twelve minutes conversing with the residents of Hell, I made my way up to the front door and knocked as loudly as possible on it. As I knocked on the door, it opened up. That was when I realized all I had to do was push the door, for it was already open. First time after a year and a half I set foot inside that house, and it felt bizarre. The home I cherished so much, the house I spent most of my time in all of a sudden seemed new to me. I could not make sense of it, but the only thing that stood out were the fifteen-step flight of stairs.

That was the only thing in that house that had not aged, that sweet, fifteen-step flight of stairs. What was once my home was shared with another family, my cousin had rented the first-floor to a lovely family to get some extra money to take care of herself. I was not allowed to go through the first-floor balcony and made my way to what was once the downstairs dining room, and I was not allowed to go to the garage where I used to play soccer with the kids from the neighborhood and where I had my first marble game with Stanley. All I was able to do was get up those fifteen stairs and hope Aunt Yaya was up there. I greeted the friendly family and gave one of their kids some candy I had bought from outside of the school then proceeded to make my way upstairs.

I could hear my cousin talking to some people upstairs, and it sounded pretty severe. I could tell there was some high energy that was being released up there. As I laid my right foot on the first step, I travelled back in time. That step took me right back to the night Yaya and her sister, Grandma Ana had their fight. At the time, I thought I was given a second chance to change things, to prevent what was going on and save the fate of that house, but in reality, I was just zoned out.

As I was in my zone, I saw my grandmother standing in that same spot, halfway through the flight of stairs as she was making her way up.

Before she could even open up her mouth to tell me some things I would never be able to understand, I interrupted her and said, "Why? Why did you have to leave so soon? Ever since I left the house I have never gotten the chance to see you again. You never come back here...no warning, no hints, nothing at all, why does it have to be like this? What have I done to deserve all of this?"

She looked at me straight in the eyes as she gave me that same, beautiful smile she gave me the last time we were on those stairs and said, "Some things you will never be able to understand."

At this point, I was mad. I was upset to the point where I felt like steam was coming off my ears. I was going to yell at her and ask her to give me a good reason for her leaving us so soon. She came down a few stairs and hugged me and said, "Come on, let's go upstairs, we are all waiting for you for the planning."

When I got out of the zone, I was between my cousin's arms as she was asking me to come up and help them plan the funeral.

I got up the stairs while wiping my eyes dry.

Chapter Fourteen

First Love Encounter

That is what my grandmother was, a shooting star. She was the brightest one, the leading shooting star. What I did not know was the fact the night when Stevenson was hoping I saw the shooting star, I did not realize it was my grandmother's. I do not believe in that theory, but Stevenson sure does, and sadly, he had proof. I cannot argue about that. Just like my godfather, her passing allowed me to meet family members I never knew existed. All my life, the only thing I wanted was a huge family. I wanted to be around them and bond with them; that was the only wish I had. I still do. Nothing beats being around a whole family. You feel protected, and love is all around even though it does not show. I have seen my friends with their families. I got jealous to the point where they would tell me I was part of their family as well, but it was not the same feeling. I wanted to be around my cousins and get in trouble together. There was nothing worse than getting your ass whooped alone after you've done something terrible. I wanted to consume the beatings with my cousins together. That way I felt like it would make more sense, it would at least be a little bit fun. It wasn't up until Stevenson showed up we shared the beatings. Before him it was just my lonely self.

I realized this was not a good way of getting to know my family. After every death in the family, I got to meet some of them, maybe that was the way it was supposed to be. Perhaps I was doomed, and death was the only way, the rare portal I could go through to fulfill my dream. That was the only door I had to go through to get what I desired the most. One thing was sure; death would be the cause of a whole new man, a whole new mindset, a more compassionate type of being that would be a part of a modern society with a mission that is yet to be accomplished. The loss of family members and loved ones was just a preparation. The worst was, however, to come; these deaths were just the tip of the iceberg. Her passing had allowed me to identify who my favorite aunt was, and I had to see Uncle Daddy again. He was not the same, for anger and rage resided in his eyes during these days. He barely talked and spent most of his days alone.

Just like Gwo Jean, we had a family gathering for the wake, but we invited some of our closest friends. The wake did not happen in the house; we did not want to deal with all the trouble random people would have caused. We had the wake at a location provided by the local morgue. It was a huge reception area, but still a part of the mortuary. There were many people there, a lot more than we had expected. It was a pretty quiet situation where the saddest tears were singing hymns and trying to wash away the depressed vibe in the building. Before the wake even began, we were asked if we wanted to see the deceased. I thought that was odd; I thought we were not supposed to take a look at the dead before the funeral, but for some reason, I thought that would bring me bad luck. Not that it would matter, everywhere I went death seemed to follow, and going in there to see the deceased would not have made a difference. Yaya sadly said yes to the request, and three of my aunts followed her through the back door. On the other hand, I did not feel ready to face such reality. Even though I knew she had passed, even though I had made my peace with the fact, I could not bring myself to see her lying there lifeless. I was not ready to face her, and I never would be.

In the back of my head, I knew the way all four of them went through that door would not be the same when they came out of it. Just like I expected, they came out different. They came out hopeless, and it seemed like they had left the most important part of themselves in that room with my grandmother. I wondered if I went in there, how I would come out. Stevenson told me maybe I would come out a "freaking human being." He might have been right. All my life I have been told I am not human based on the fact I act differently and think differently than most people do. That was not even the worst case; my ways got a lot worse as I made my way to Heaven. My personality became more unique; to some people, I would become weirder than I was before. It got to the point where I even considered myself not to be human. I believed myself to be the darkest person alive, one with no soul, one with no heart. For some reason I lost the ability to sympathize up until I made it to Heaven. I did not want to put on a mask as some other people did. I wanted to be myself, but that seemed to get some people upset. I could not play pretend. I had been asked to, but those people had no idea how difficult it was to pretend you were sad. It is not something you can choose to be, my best guess is, it just happens.

"*Mourir aupres de mon amour,*" that is what was playing before anybody got the chance to say something they needed to let out. That was a song by my favorite Greek singer Demis Roussos. A reasonably sad song that would get your tears coming out unwillingly, a song I found to be very relaxing. After savoring the song maybe thirty people had been feeling very sad about, the time had come for family and friends to say a couple of words about my grandmother. I did not say anything, I could not face it, and I did not want that situation to be real. Yaya did not say anything either. She sat right next to me and kept on shaking her legs and humming some gospel songs.

To calm her down, I put my head on her lap as she caresses my head and listening to my other aunts and favorite uncle give their eulogies. I could feel her teardrops hitting my face as she tried to wipe them away.

I put my arms around her waist and kept my head on her belly as she kept on playing with my hair.

At some point the crying stopped, and one of my aunts, my favorite one, came to me and told me: "They are about to close. Is there anything, like anything on your mind you want to say? It could be anything nice she had done for you or something you admired about her."

Although I was a timid young man, I did not want to share the good memories I had with her, especially how she had helped me find my way through my first love's heart. I would go past being shy just for her; I would do anything in the world to be with her one last time and enjoy that previous beautiful smile she gave me halfway through the fifteen stairs, but sharing her memories was not one of those things I was willing to do.

I did not want the good memories I shared with her to be out in the open. I did not want them to be part of all the other ones that were shared in that room that night. I kept them to myself, but one of those great memories I had with her showed me what it meant to fall in love with someone. When I was eleven, I had my eyes on a girl who was also a resident of Hell. She was not my first girlfriend, but she was the first woman in my entire life who made me feel what feeling something for someone was. It was a strange feeling, and I had no idea who she was or where she was from. All I knew was she was a very stunning woman. I called her "Angel" even though I had no idea who she was. I did not need to know her name; to me, Angel was her name. What I did not re-alize was the fact she was the girlfriend of a guy I admired a lot. He was my hero; he would defend me whenever kids in the neighborhood were picking on me. I did not know him that well, but we had a little bond. It was not a strong one, and it was not weak also. He would always look around the house to find me so he could say hi, and I would be on the second-floor balcony almost every morning at six trying to catch a glimpse of him going to school to call him out loud and greet him. In a sense, I could say we were cool mates.

Angel had unlocked my ability to fall in love within seconds. She was just that important part of my life I needed to experience. All it took was one look at her when she was buying something from the store that separated the house from the river. I was standing on the upstairs balcony when I first laid eyes on her. My heart jumped out of my chest and dropped all the way downstairs and kept on bouncing around in the hope of her picking it up and stopping it from destroying itself. Sadly, she did not do such a thing, and I was glad she did not because I wanted to see her again. I wanted to feel the same way again. The second time I saw her, the same thing happened, but this time it was different. I felt the need to say something to her, but what exactly could I say to such a beauty to get her attention? That was my very first love challenge. I could not bring myself to say anything to her; I was speechless. I got paralyzed to such a ravishing creature.

That was when I realized I needed help to gain access to her heart. The house next door was occupied by a little girl who used to go to the same school as me, and I used to talk to her almost every day. She was the only person who could help me accomplish such a mission given the fact she was Angel's friend. I had no idea what love was or how to approach a woman, and I was too scared to talk to any women who was not too close to me at the time, especially the ones who trusted me. I guess in a way I was afraid of being rejected, and I also was scared of saying something that would have a negative effect on such a beauty's day. My friend suggested I write her a note, more like a letter. That was my first writing assignment. The fact I had to write about how I genuinely felt about that girl already shows how crazy my feelings for her were. I had written before, but not for this particular reason. This letter was the first thing I signed with a special pen, which at the time I referred to as "my heart."

After pouring my heart out on that sheet of paper, I went straight to my friend's house and handed it over to her. She promised me she would give it to her, and she also told Angel I was in love with her. That was not a wise move. I did not want her to pay attention to me whenever she was buying something from that store. Every time she came around after receiving that letter, she was always looking up in hope to catch a glimpse of me. Sometimes our eyes would meet, and when that happened I would leave and go straight to the garage and savor such an experience. As time went by, and our eyes kept on meeting, I would get lost in hers and wished to stay in there until the end of time. I would keep staring at her until she no longer existed in the real world, but in my mind she would be present. Sometimes I wish she had said something to me so I could respond, but she never did, and I never got the chance to say a word to her. All I could say was at least she knew my heart was hers for a moment.

After such a failure I had given up, and as time flew by my feelings for her started to diminish. That was one thing they do not tell you about love, the fact it fades as time grows old. I did not see her the same anymore, and I did not care if I saw her or not. That fire was not burning the same anymore in my heart. One day I went to my friend's house and asked her about how Angel was doing. She told me she was doing fine and she had a boyfriend the whole time I was going crazy for her. That was not going to change the way I felt for her, and I did not care if she had a boyfriend or not, I just wanted her magical beauty to ignite the fire that was once burning deep inside my soul. When my friend told me the boyfriend was the guy who was protecting me all along, I was shocked as my heart had skipped a couple of beats. Before the girl next door gave me the sad news, she told me Angel had ordered her to ask me for a picture of mine. I was wondering why would she need a picture of me; maybe she had sensed my feeling was going away. Perhaps she realized the fire was fading away, so she was trying to figure out a way to reignite it and make it ten times brighter than it was before. Without hesitating, I pulled out my Spider-Man wallet and took one of the small pictures out and hand it over to her.

"You are not going to write anything on the back of that picture...It is a nice one. I like the smile," my friend said to me.

I looked down and said back to her, "I have already written her a letter, and I had no response, what is the point of writing on the back of the photo?"

She looked back at me all smiling and left me standing outside of her house. Part of me felt like she was playing since she gave me that smile, but what did I have to lose. I had lost interest in Angel. I was hoping the photo would make her talk to me, but that photo had another purpose, a very confusing and hurtful one.

One beautiful afternoon, I could hear my friend getting an ass-whooping from her uncle. Her mother was sick, so she was not able to take care of the situation. She asked her brother to do so. The ass-whooping was intense; it was so intense I had to go to her house and see for myself and figure out the reason behind such a beating. Once I got there, I could see the uncle going crazy on her behind, and as soon as she saw me, the crying stopped, and she started smiling. The smile seemed to upset the uncle even more as he hit her way harder than he was before.

I got confused. I could not figure out what was going on, and I felt terrible for my friend, for she was crying and sweating profusely from the beating.

As I was going to ask what was going on, the maid told me to stop. "Wait, do you know something?" I asked her.

She answered, "I do not know anything, kid. That is none of my concern. Just do whatever you please, sir."

That was fairly odd, and from the way she stopped me I felt like I had something to do with her getting her ass whooped. I went to her living room where her mother was resting in the hope of finding out what was going on, but her facial expression told me to get the hell out of her house, and so I did. That kept me up all night trying to figure out the meaning behind such a look. Her mother was nice to everybody, especially me, but I sensed she had changed from the way she looked at me that day. She was different now, and every time she saw me, she gave me that judgmental Haitian facial expression.

The next day, I went over her house and saw her taking care of the wounds from the beatings.

"Here, let me help you with that" I said to her as I took the hydrogen peroxide from her hand.

I helped her with the treatment, and as soon as I was going to ask her about what was behind such a beating, she said, "You do not want my mother to see you in here. She is pretty pissed at you. She thought you were that nice, respectable kid, but you turned out to be someone else, and she does not want me to talk to you anymore."

I gave her the sad eyes as I said, "What! What have I done? And I am still that person. I am still that type of kid! I did not do anything wrong."

Tears ran down her face when she looked up in hope to keep them from dripping and blurted out, "It was all my fault, she had seen it, I am sorry."

I gently put my left arm around her neck and softly said, "Sorry for what? Whatever it is, I already forgive you before you even had the chance to think about doing it. You are my friend, and I will do anything to help you. Now what did you do? Tell me. It will be okay."

I did forgive her that day, but I just wished I had not pushed her into telling me about what she had done. After wiping the tears off her face, she went on by saying Angel did not ask for the photo. She did that so she could have a picture of me. I found that to be ridiculous, and I had no words to say after hearing that, but that was not the real reason behind it. That would be far too simple a reason for a girl to get beaten like that. The worst decision she had made was the fact she had written something on the back of the photo as if it were me who wrote it. It was a beautiful poem, and it made perfect sense with the way I was smiling in the picture. During this era, a girl was not supposed to be in a relationship or having a man in her life, especially if they were that young. Growing up under a Haitian roof, I would say the proper time for you to get engaged with someone or to even think about dating someone would be when you left your parents' home, and that rarely happened considering the economic situation of the country. That was when I realized I had made a fool out of myself. I just got up and left as she begged me to stay a little longer.

I did not know how I felt that day. Confused would not be a good enough way to describe such a feeling. I had questioned myself that day, and still asked myself why do people like to suffer? Why don't they go after what they want instead of hoping it will come to them? Of course, going after something you want does not necessarily mean you will get it, but at least you have tried. I kept on wondering why she did not just tell me she liked me. She could have just said it, and I would be glad to give her the photo. At least I would know I was being treated like that for a good reason, not for something I did not do. Before I knew it, the whole neighborhood knew about the incident. Even my literature tutor knew about it, for he taunted me that night.

It was a very long day, and it was probably the worst I ever had. I was supposed to meet with my tutor at home, but I went to the only place where I could clear my mind, that soccer field. By the time I got home, night had welcome itself to the neighborhood. Yaya told me the tutor came in when I was out, so he said to her I could come over to his house around nine to go over my school work. I did precisely that, and I wished I had not. I went to his house and saw him standing next to his front door with that mysterious smile of his. I had never seen him smiling like that, but that was not too concerning to me. I had bigger fish to fry. As we went through some work, he asked me a question about my homework, but my mind was too full; I did not know the answer.

He looked at me and laughed evilly and said, "How could you have known? You are too busy trying to get with a woman."

Without hesitating, I grabbed my books and my backpack and left. That was the last time I saw that tutor.

As for Farah, my best friend who had kept the photo that was supposed to go to Angel, she did not take it too well after I left her house, and to be honest I did not care how she felt at the time. I was an ignorant fool who just kept on thinking she just lied and that was the only reason I needed to be pretty pissed at her even though she was sorry. All this time, the only thing I was looking for was right under my nose, and I could not even get a whiff of it. Instead, I was hoping to climb a mountain that was forbidden for me to even think about. That was the end of our friendship. We stopped talking and stopped seeing each other. Not only had I lost a friend, but I had gained the evil part of my heart, and that made me one of the real residents of Hell.

The quest for love did not stop there. I was yet to find my better half. I was, however, to seek another soul to occupy that lonely and love-hungry body. It was not an easy task, but with the help of the Almighty, my Grandmother Ana, it was possible, and that was my first success when it came to finding love. It was a year after the photo incident I had a peculiar dream, and I would later realize the best relationship was the one where you were not a participant. Just like Angel, my heart would find that fire again, except this time it was burning to the point where everybody could see it. That fire was loud, and you could spot it from far away due to the heavy smoke that was dancing on the top of it. Love would have a whole new meaning to me as my grandmother told me the secret to gaining access to the heart of the girl I admired the most in Hell.

CHAPTER FIFTEEN

HELL'S LOVE

It was not a secret like the deepest one I possess. It was more like an everyday type of thing we are all supposed to do. We ignored it to blend in with others instead of embracing it and letting it blossom. I knew I had to embrace it, but society would not allow me to do so. They would think differently of me. My grandmother, when I was twelve years of age, helped me to gain the key to a sweet woman's heart, and it was one of the best feelings I have ever had. Naturally, Haitian parents do not help their kids with such a thing, but I think my grandmother was fine with helping me just because I was a boy and because I guess I had no man around to show me how to get it done. I think in a way she was afraid I would turn into someone else given the fact I was around women all the time. If you were to ask your Haitian parents to help you with such a quest, you would probably get your ass beat, or they would cuss you out, or even send you to the countryside for some time to think, which was what happened to my cousin.

Hell was where wonders happened pretty much every day. There was always something going on, and for me, the first wonder that happened to me there was laying my eyes on Thami. At the time, I had no clue what love was, and to me, she was love itself. When I first fixed my eyes on her, I felt like that was not the first time. It felt like a déjà vu. Stevenson seemed to disagree with me, but I knew I had seen her before. The first time I saw her, I knew she looked familiar. Not only because of her beauty but because of her soft voice and the way she walked, it was all perfection. I used to have a dream pretty much every other day. Sometimes I remembered every detail, and sometimes I did not, but it came back to me at some point during the day. In Haiti, dreams mean a lot to most of the population. For example, if one had a vision about marrying someone, that dream meant that one of the two would die soon. That was one of the popular dreams in Haiti. Dreams even helped some people win the lottery, and because of that, one of the guys with whom I used to hang out always came around and asked me about what I dreamed about last night.

There would be a huge, brick wall, and I would try to break through it and make it to the other side, but it seemed impenetrable. I would try to climb over it, but it seemed to be getting higher and higher every time I tried to make it to the other side. I would kick it and sometimes throw some rocks at it, but it did not even sound like it was getting hit by the stone. That was the dream I kept on having, and every time I woke up from that dream, I would be sweaty and felt like I was trying to take that wall down in real life. I had been trying to figure out the meaning behind that dream for days, but there were no answers. I did not believe dreams were supposed to mean anything, but I was just curious because I had the same one over and over again. I explained it to Stevenson, but that was not very helpful. He suggested the next night I should put a pickaxe under the bed, and that way I could use it in the dream to demolish that wall. I did no such thing; I went to the guy who seemed to be interested in my visions and told him about it so he could win the lottery. That was when I realized my dream had no real meaning behind it.

It was not up until a few weeks later I was able to tear that wall down. I finally asked my aunt to explain to me what that dream meant.

As I told her about it, she held my hand and said, "Do you pray before you go to bed?"

I looked at her and gave her a creepy smile as I realized I had found the secret to tearing that wall down. That night before I even got on the bed, I knelt before it and had a five-minute prayer, and it felt good. I had not prayed in ages, and after I did that I felt at peace. I felt more than ready to bust that wall down. I did not have that dream that night, and I had not had it for a while, but I kept on praying every night and asked God to allow me to have that dream again.

A few weeks later, the prayers had become a habit of mine. I just kept on praying and hoping I would get another shot at the dream, but it still did not happen. At that point, I just gave up, but I still kept on praying about other stuff. One night I was too tired from playing soccer all day with the kids from the Hell. I came home, took a shower, and just jumped on the bed without even thinking about praying. I slept soundly that night as I was facing that wall again. That wall was different from the previous ones. It was taller and green, and it looked more robust than the previous one as well. It was way different because this time I did not have to worry about breaking it down or climbing right over it. I could use the door that was at the center of it and make it to the other side. The problem was, I did not know what was waiting for me on the other side. I did not think I was ready to see what was waiting for me back there. That door would reveal the most precious thing I had ever seen, and it would just project it right in front of me. I opened the door, and Hell had shown itself.

I found myself back in the same neighborhood but at a precise location. There was a river, not the small one that was facing my childhood home, that one was about three minutes away from my house, and every weekend Stevenson and I would go there and swim around with the other kids from the neighborhood. We all loved that river because it was deep, and we could do almost anything in there, but some of the grown-ups would defecate on the water so we could get out and let them wash their clothes. I found myself over there in the dream, and I saw the same girl, the girl with the beautiful black and blue dress. She was washing her clothes and also "*Tire lobe*" in the water. That was a way the kids would hit the water with their palm, and it would make a sound like you were playing the drum, and she was pretty good at it. That was the first official time I had met my first love. In that dream, I was able to get a good sight of her. I saw her there that one day in real life, but backflipping with my friends was more important at that time.

I would later see her again, but to me, that would be the very first time since I did not get a good look at her at that river. I was hanging out on the balcony, sipping milk in a wine glass with Stevenson and another kid. She was wearing the same dress, and she had a lovely gold necklace around her neck. It probably had her name on it. I did not have a good look at it, but it shone as the sunrays reflected on it. She was at that *boutik* trying to buy some cooking goods. As I stood there with the milk in my left hand, my jaw dropped as my eyes met hers. Time stopped instantly, and her beauty just added a new flavor to the day. Suddenly, it was not as hot as it was before I saw her. It was cold, and I desperately needed her body warmth to keep mine at average temperature. Her face was angelic; it glowed as the sunlight rested on it and her eyes, so innocent, I got lost in them trying to escape my evil ways and let her realize how much she had meant to me that very moment. My heart was already hers, and my mind was hers to do anything she pleased. I suddenly became her genie; her wishes were my command. I thought I knew what love was when I had seen Angel for the first time, but at this very moment I realized how wrong I was. Not only did I feel what love was at that time, but I found it, and it was fifteen staircases away from me to take a chance at it.

"Do you have something up there? Have you lost something? Can I help you?" my cousin interrupted the most precious moment I was having as she screamed at Thami. She had caught Thami staring upstairs for the longest time, and that seemed to have upset my cousin in a way, except I was even more upset at her. I had been kicked out from that magical place I was enjoying as my eyes left Thami's. Yaya seemed to understand what was going on as she laughed and asked my cousin to relax and let the beauty have the most delightful day of her life. I was hoping she would look back. I tried everything to get her attention. I said some dumb stuff, talked out loud...none of that worked. Instead, I witnessed her black and blue dress leaving my sight as the wind blew it away, and her beauty was fading away as she headed back to her home.

When the dark hours said hello to the neighborhood, I could not sleep because every time I shut my eyes I could see nothing but her, and I was afraid going to sleep was going to take such a beautiful picture out of my head. That was when I realized I would need some help trying to win such a perfect heart. I would first talk to Stevenson, but that was not a very wise choice.

That night, as sleep was playing hide and seek with me, I reached out to Stevenson after Yaya had made us some hot chocolate mixed with some powdered milk. As we sat at that table, I turned my back to Stevenson and quickly started a conversation with him. I turned my back because what I was about to discuss with him was important, and sometimes Stevenson tended to be a clown and make me laugh whenever I was serious. I wanted him to hear me out and come up with a solution.

With my back still turned, I said to him, "Yo, Stevenson, did you see that girl today at Nicole's boutik?"

I then heard him put his goblet down and say slowly, "What are you doing? Turn around."

"Are you going to take me seriously?" I said to him with a severe tone.

"You have not even started telling me anything. How do I know If I am to be serious or not?" he asked.

"I don't know, man, just do not laugh, just be serious," I said to him as I turned back.

I could see that stupid grin on his face, and I knew he would be laughing before I even had the chance to ask him if he saw that beautiful girl who was at the boutik earlier.

He went about by saying: "There were many girls buying stuff at Nicole's today. Which one? Was she the one who got your attention so much you spilled your freaking milk all over my T-shirt?"

I said yes as he told me her name was Thami, and she was living right next to the soccer field. He went on by saying how lucky I was because Thami's sister was his best friend. I asked him to help me to talk to her, but he was not very helpful, for he was too childish. He told me to let her know I loved her, but that was not the case for me. For me, women were that blazing hot erupted volcano I did not want to approach. I was scared of them; I was afraid of disappointing them. I told Stevenson this was not an option, I could never pull this off, and that was when he had said to me he could not do anything else for me because he did not want to jeopardize his friendship with Thami's sister.

What I did not know was the fact my grandmother was to visit us the next day, and a couple of days after her arrival I would do the impossible. When Ana showed up I was surprised because I had no idea she was coming, and my aunt wanted to surprise me. I was more than surprised, and I had hugged my grandmother with all my might that day. I quickly took her handbag and gave it to Stevenson so he could bring them upstairs, and I took care of the luggage. The best part of my grandmother coming to visit us was the unpacking of her luggage, and that did not happen up until nine or ten at night. During the day, we talked about family matters and ask how the rest of them over there were doing. Ana went on about how much I had grown and who I reminded her of as I was getting older. She said I look more and more like my mother. She took her time to look at me and ask me all sorts of questions, but I was desperately waiting for her to ask me the right question. When the night hit there was no electricity, and we had to use our kerosene lamp to go through the gifts my grandmother had brought us.

The balcony smelled like a clothing store. It had the scent of brand-new clothes and shoes. Plastics wraps were all over the floor and gift wraps as well. It was the time when the house was complete. That was the true meaning of what happiness was to me. There was no better feeling than knowing your loved ones were around when you are going to bed, and I could not wait for the next day to spend all my time with her and share everything she had missed from the last time she had left us.

That night we fell asleep to telling jokes and riddles. We would sometimes talk a little bit about politics, and most of the times I would fall asleep to the humming of old songs my grandmother used to listen to as a young girl. Two days after her arrival, she asked me the question I wanted her to ask me. She was sitting on the balcony that connected to the flight of stairs, and the level of boredom was intense for both of us. I wanted to go to the soccer field, but I also wanted to be around my grandmother, for I had missed her so much. I was sitting right next to her as she looked around and enjoyed the hot weather.

She could sense I was bored, and she said to me, "Hey, you, come here...let me have a bite of your belly, *Ti Mireille*."

I slowly got up as I waited for her to say she had changed her mind. I pulled up my T-shirt, and she bit me right on my belly and I would giggle. She laughed so hard Yaya asked her if she was okay. After that sweet bite, she told me to sit on her lap, and that was when the question I long waited for came out.

◆ ◆ ◆

"I know you are all grown, you probably think you are, but in my eyes, you are still my little grandson. I have heard about the photo situation, and to be frank, I do not believe it was intentional, but my question is, do you have a girlfriend?"

The sky had opened up, and God Himself had come down and blessed her heart for asking me such a question. If you are a Haitian kid, the best thing to do was to think twice about such a question and lie in the smartest way possible to avoid the meanest ass whooping. Sometimes our parents would trick us like that by asking us such a question, but that was not the case for me. I was more than ready to answer her truthfully and faithfully, and at that time I had more faith in my grandmother than I did in God. I was as calm as possible when I was getting ready to answer her question, and I could sense she could not wait to hear what I had to say. I looked right at her persuasive eyes and told her I loved her, and a kiss on her cheek followed.

After the kiss, I put my right arm on her shoulders and answered her question by blurting out those same words, "Well, I do not have a girl-friend at the moment, but I think I love someone."

"You think, or you know?" she replied as I scratched my head in con-fusion. "Do you even know what love is?" she asked me as I was still confused.

I said to her with my right arm still resting on her shoulders, "I know what love is. I saw it a few days ago, and I believe she is love herself."

Not too many people would take their time to listen to what a twelve-ear-old boy had to say, especially about something he knew nothing about, love. Ana was different; she took her time hearing me out, and that boosted my confidence to get what I believed would make me the happi-est kid in Hell. After I told her about the girl, she told me to get up, and I did. My eyes were still locked into hers as she stayed quiet for about a minute. It was a bit awkward, but I survived it. She finally let some words out of her mouth by asking me what I wanted to do about this girl. I told her I did not know. I let her know I did not know how to talk to her, and I certainly did not know how to win her heart.

"You said she is love herself. Don't you want to go out there and catch it?" she asked me.

I replied by saying: "Yes, I do, but I will need some help, some ad-vice on how to perform such a trick."

"It is not that complicated, you know. Just go and be yourself, talk to that girl and be her friend," my grandmother whispered because she did not want Aunt Yaya to hear our secret conversation.

To me, that was the biggest challenge I had to face. Not only was I scared to talk to her, but I was terrified I might disappoint her, and I would not get another chance at gazing on such a beauty, I did not want to lose that privilege. I told my grandmother I did not believe I was the only guy to see how beautiful she was. There were probably thousands of other guys in *Hell* who had the same mission as me. How could I compete to be the sole proprietor of such a pure heart? If it were a race, I would be the very last guy to make it.

My grandmother just insisted on me being myself, and that seemed to be impossible as I said to her, "But, grandma...I am not as good-looking as these other guys, God took his time creating those guys. They are cute, they are handsome, and me, I am just that!"

She had a grin on her face as I said those words to her with my head facing the floor. My grandmother pulled my chin up and went, "You think you are ugly, *Ti Mireille*?"

I said with the softest voice ever, "I know I am; I have been told so."

I waited for her to tell me otherwise, but she did not, and I was glad she did not. Instead of being fake and telling me I was more handsome than all of the other guys with whom I had to compete, she held my face with her soft palm and said slowly, "Then be ugly. Be yourself and go catch love. She is waiting."

That was all I needed to hear as I was preparing to go on my mission. After conversing with my grandmother, I went back to the other balcony and waited for hours to catch a glimpse of love. I even missed having dinner with the family trying to catch a glimpse of her. Food was not necessary at the time, and *love* was all I could think about, she was the only thing that was occupying my mind at that time. As I was getting ready to leave the balcony because it was getting dark, love had made her apparition, and I got lost. I was happier than a dog waiting to be thrown a chicken bone, except I had no tail to show such excitement. I needed no light to see such beauty—pure Caribbean beauty even on her worst day. Even when she was mad, she was still the prettiest woman I had ever seen in Hell, and that night something seemed to upset her.

She did not look the same as I saw her the first time, and I know I had to do something to get her attention. Lucky for me, she looked up again, even though my cousin was telling her to do otherwise. She looked up, and our eyes had met for the second time, and my heart melted. I loved her to the point where when I looked at her it hurts, and that was the best pain anybody on the planet could ever ask to feel. She was wearing no makeup, just pure beauty at its finest. As our eyes met, I froze, and my brain kept on telling me to do something.

I waved at her, she smiled, and she waved back.

That night, I felt like I have found the meaning behind everything, I have found the meaning of life. The girl I loved so much had waved back at me! That was just a miracle, but I did not believe in miracles at that time. It was safe to say this was the very first one I had experienced. I no longer felt like a boy like many of the grown-ups from Hell would call me. I felt like a man. I felt like I could do anything that night, and I was more than ready to go out there and talk to her and let her know how flammable my love for her was, but that did not happen up until the next day. I could not sleep that night, and I just kept on picturing her face while she was waving back at me. She did not just wave back. I made her smile, and that smile was one for the books. I looked everywhere to find one exactly like that, and I would do anything to see it again, but I could not find it anywhere. That smile was one of her characteristics; it was the most important way you could describe what real satisfaction was. That smile could open the gates of Hades and restore all the lost ones; it could make you smile even in your darkest hour.

The next day when I woke up from a two hours sleep, I was pretty tired, but the most important thing to do that day was talk to *love*. I was so happy that morning I even forgot to give my grandmother her morning kiss and Yaya those hugs where I rocked her left and right and kissed her afterward. I went straight downstairs and got ready to start the day. As usual, I started the day with a plate of spaghetti, Caribbean style, two eggs, and a glass of fresh-squeezed orange juice. As I sat on the downstairs balcony enjoying the view outside, one of Thami's big brothers threw me a piece of paper. I thought he was acting like a jerk, for he was most of the time, but this time he had given me the best way to gain access to his sister's heart. I was about to throw the piece of paper to the trash can, but Stevenson told me there was something written on it, and I should check it out. I was speechless. It was a note from *love*, and the best part was the way she signed the note. Instead of her name, she signed it with her number.

The message went like this: *Thank you for making me smile yesterday.*

I held on to that piece of paper for the longest time up until I had lost it while moving to Purgatory. That note had become my favorite prayer, and I would read it every time I went to bed and every morning when I woke up. That day, when I received that note, I knew what I had to do. I knew I had to call her, and that way it would be a lot easier to express my feeling without being lost in her eyes. I could not wait for night time, and I knew she could not stop checking her phone in the hope I would call. That was one of the first longest days of my life, and I knew it would be worth it to wait until nighttime to set my feelings free. Before I knew it, the day had escaped and the night had introduced itself to the neighborhood, and the level of nervousness was off the chart.

I was sweating for no reason just thinking about how I would start this conversation. I once again asked Stevenson for help, and again, he was not very helpful. He believed when it came to talking to a woman that was an easy task, but to me it was a very long trigonometry problem I had to solve. It felt like I was to answer every bit of challenge that resided inside that math book I used to hate so much. As I was nervous, I went to my cousin's room in the hope of finding the letters her boyfriend had sent her, but I could not spot any of them. As I was leaving her room all sad and hopeless, Stevenson stopped me and handed me a letter, and that letter boosted my confidence that night.

It was a letter my cousin's boyfriend had written to her, and it was a well-written one too. You could feel the love while reading that letter, and it was very romantic and mighty. I had no idea how Stevenson managed to get his hands on that letter, but that was not important that night. I studied that letter in about forty-five minutes and made my way up to the roof because I did not want anybody to hear what I was about to say. I needed my space, but Stevenson was following me everywhere I went, so I chose the only place I knew he could not access. There were no staircases to get up there. We had to use a ladder, and after I had used it, I pulled it up and gave him the middle finger as he was watching me with his sad eyes. I lay on my back watching the stars worshiping the giant luminous moon as I dialed her number.

She answered by saying, "I thought you were never going to call. What took you so long?"

I laughed nervously as she spat out those words.

With the letter still folded in my left hand, I responded to her by saying, "I did not think my call was that important to you, and if I knew, I'd have called you the second I received your note."

After I said those words, I realized Stevenson had given her my number because it was sort of strange that she would answer the phone like that without knowing it was me. The conversation went well; it went so well I did not even need that letter. I took it all folded up and put it on my back pocket. The only thing I needed was to be myself, and that was the one thing I did that night. I was the ugliest guy in Hell that night.

Just like my grandmother said, being my true self had granted me the way to such a woman's heart. We talked for almost two hours that night, and it was the most fabulous night ever. My heart was pounding, and I could feel the heartbeat through my toes. It was as if she was standing right next to me. After those two long hours, I got down from the roof and met Stevenson who was still down there waiting for me.

When I got down, he asked me how it went. I looked at him all serious for a second, then I lifted him with joy surrounding me and said out loud, "I got my first girlfriend. I was accepted, brother, she accepted me!"

He begged me to put him down, and so I did. He gave a pat on the back and told me, "I gave her your number. I was trying to help."

I took his hand and shook it then said, "You did good, man. You did good, and I thank you."

What I did not know was what I signed up for that night. I had no idea I had signed up for my very first heartbreak when it was time for her to leave me all alone in Hell so she could find her own Purgatory.

Through my grandmother, all was possible, and that was the best gift, the best memory she had given me, and for that, I was and will always be very grateful. She taught me the secret of how to catch love, and was I successful? I would say so. She was my guardian angel and still, she is guiding me through her teachings and her methods. How could one forget about her? How could you miss her? That is impossible, at least for me it is. You cannot miss something that is always with you. Her love is all that matters to me, and every day I feel it. I do not know how she did it, but she had the power to make you feel loved even if she was not around.

After her passing, I could still feel such love, and it was irreplaceable. Death is not the end. It could be the end for some, but it is essential how you leave the loved ones behind. Were there great memories? Because those are the ones that stay. Everything else vanishes. Those are the ones that keep the deceased alive in your mind, in your heart. Have you showed the loved ones how much you loved them?,Have you made them feel loved even in your absence? That's the key. That is the secret to be immortal. Appreciate every single one of your loved ones and accept them as they are because there is nothing better than being who you are, and you have to be that at best. I knew I was loved because I felt it and am still feeling it, but one thing I knew and I appreciated, that one thing I was sure of was the fact not only was I loved, but most importantly I was accepted. I was allowed to be the person I honestly am.

THE NEIGHBORHOODS (RUELLE MICASA)

PART III

HEAVEN

CHAPTER SIXTEEN

FROM HELL TO HEAVEN

Hell was where it all started, and sadly, that was not where it ended. If it were up to me, this would be the place where I would love the end to happen, but that would also mean these writings would not be as essential. That was the place I hope one day I would be able to take my last breath. That was the place where I took my first step as a Haitian, and this was and will always be my home. You are doomed, some would say to me, for being too proud to be a resident of Hell, and because of it, I have found a new way of living life. It was tough, but I had the best of times in there, and I met the only angel who got lost in there. If it were not for Hell, I would not be the person I am today. Purgatory was like Hell's little brother. He was the brother who annoyed you all day and gave you a hard time every now and then, but he would still care for you, and sometimes he would blame himself so you could escape the worst whooping.

My time in Purgatory was short, shorter than the ones I have spent in Hell, but it was the place where I had found a little bit of myself. It was the place where I learned about what it meant to be human, what it truly meant to be fair to others. If I had to compare both of these neighborhoods to some people, Hell would be me during the time I was living there because I was that ignorant, arrogant, and a self-serving type of individual. Purgatory, on the other hand, would be Stevenson, the kind of person who, besides all the unpleasant treatments, still figures out a way to see the good in people. He was always the one to stand up for you in your time of need. He would even fight your battles for you. The fact of the matter is both of these neighborhoods prepared me for what was to come in Heaven. It was not up until I made it to Heaven I had realized why I had to leave the previous neighborhoods, and that was when I had also understood how much that saying meant to me, "Everything happens for a reason," and truthfully, leaving Hell had a real reason behind it. I might not have had a clue on why I had to abandon such a beautiful neighborhood, and I also thought it was a punishment, but in reality, it indeed was a blessing.

Leaving Hell was hard, but not as hard as leaving Purgatory. I would choose Hell over Purgatory anytime, but one thing stood out for Purgatory, the memories I wished I had in Hell. I had some good memories in Hell, but not as pleasant as Purgatory's, and the majority of the memories I had in Hell were the bad ones. In a way, that was one of the essences of Hell. If I were to experience what I had experienced in Purgatory right there in Hell, there would be no need for Purgatory. I would go straight to Heaven from Hell, and that was one of the reasons everything happens for a reason. My soul would not need to be purified, and I would be ready to go and face that extraordinary event I was destined to experience.

Purgatory was not the same after my grandmother's passing. It was like the neighborhood had been reborn, and all its joy was taken away from it. My aunt was not the same, and in a way, I was not the same as well. After the funeral, I tended to go back to the same old ways I used to practice when I was a Hell resident, but thanks to Purgatory, I had learned how to make sacrifices. I do believe people can change, but not entirely. You will still inherit your old ways, and the only thing that matters is the power within you to hold these old ways from coming back into the improved person you became. That was my case. I had been tested so many times in Purgatory, but only one thing stood out, the fact that this neighborhood had forged both my heart and soul into a whole new purified body, and because of that I have earned the greatest gift ever. I have received the gift of resisting against old habits. I have learned how to control myself against any temptation that comes in different forms.

Purgatory had started to lose its flavor, and the truth was it would never be the same anymore. That was that neighborhood's way of telling me my time was up and I was ready to make it to the next one. I did not think that I was prepared to move again. It was too soon, and I was not willing to do the same heavy lifting I did back in Hell. I was too comfortable in Purgatory, I wanted to stay, but the neighborhood did not want to keep me any longer. It was time for me to leave and make way for someone else to enjoy it and have a chance at finding the best version of themselves. That was the place where I had experienced what losing someone close to you was like. Even though it did not hurt like it did some other people, it taught me my only mission in life with the loved ones. It is to enjoy them while they are alive and create the best of memories. How could I ever be ready to leave such a place? It was almost like I was born there, and part of me would always be there even though Hell was the best place in the whole world. Leaving this community made me realize how bad of a person I used to be, and that was one of the challenges I had to face in life.

The bell had rung, and before I knew it, it was time for me to kiss Purgatory goodbye. I do not remember what the day was. If I had to guess, I would say it was a Saturday. It was nighttime, and we were loading Aunt Cleante's friend's truck with our belongings so we could get going and settle in Heaven. Just like in Hell, I was wondering why do we have to move? But unlike Hell, there was no family drama, and there was no fight. The real reason behind the moving was the fact Aunt Yaya had a lot of bad memories in this house and some other religious issues. Some things she could not be a part of, she could not sit there and worship God in a place where some people were participating in some other activities. Once again, just like when it was time for me to leave Hell, I had to make a tough decision. I had to decide whether or not I should stay or follow my aunt to Heaven. I had made the right choice, and it was a wise one. Otherwise, I would not be here today. I did not lose any sleep when I was making that decision. It was the easiest one, but leaving behind the new friends I had made was the toughest.

◆ ◆ ◆

Heaven was not too far away from Purgatory. If I had to guess, I would say it was probably eight to ten minutes away if you were walking. That would be the reason I had bought that silver BMX bicycle to make the trips a little bit easier when I decided to go back and visit the residents of Purgatory. Heaven was not different from the other neighborhoods, except I had to meet some new people and try to get to know them. That was not too successful. Most of Heaven's residents were old. There were just a few teenagers like me, and they usually kept to themselves, and that would be the case of me developing such love for loneliness. I was lonely in there, not because nobody wanted to be around me, but because I started to think a lot more now. I needed some alone time to come up with some good writings. I began to grow into a different type of person. I would spend most of the times in my room writing a piece or reading some books.

I never thought at some point in my life we would be renting a house from someone else, not because I thought I was better than anyone else, but because I always had the feeling everything would go back to normal. I was hoping one day I will go back to Hell and live the rest of my life in my childhood home we owned. That was not the case. That house we rented in Heaven was no different from the one we had in Hell. It was a two-story house with a balcony. There was no running water, but we did have a well in the garage, and that would be the fun part of the house. Whenever anybody needed water I would be asked to use my long and skinny arms to use the rope that was tied into a five-gallon white bucket and pull out some water for the people. That was pretty much my job over there, and I loved it! My job was also to keep it locked all the time because there were kids around.

We were not renting the whole house. The landlord was living upstairs with his family. He was a lovely guy, very religious, and sometimes he would teach me some verses from the Bible. I would say he was the only Haitian dad I had met who was not too strict because I never saw him being mad at his kids or whooping them. He had two kids, a boy, and a girl, and a beautiful wife who was as lovely as he was. Until this day, I remember him asking me this question, "Which way would you go through, the narrow road or the wide one?"

When it came to him, you did not know how to answer a question properly, and you had to be very careful answering his questions. I told him I would take the wide one, given the fact he asked me the question in English. I did not understand English that well at that time, but I could manage. I did appreciate the subject, but my answer seemed to be wrong to him. It was pretty obvious everybody would like to take the wide road. The wide one is more spacious, and you would feel more comfortable traveling in it. It was an ethical question, and I should have thought about it for a long time before answering it. At some point I felt it would not matter if I had picked the narrow one, he would have still told me I gave him the wrong answer.

"I will give you one more chance to answer this question right," he said slowly to me as the wind was playing with his gray moustache. I stood by my answer, which he seemed to like, but still he told me it was the wrong one. He told me the narrow one is the best, and I asked him why. He would say the wider one led to Hell because it was too comfortable, it was too easy to walk by, and nothing came that easy in life, and if it did, it would lead to chaos and madness. At that point I was stunned, and I was glad I chose the wider one because I would like to go back to Hell. That was the best of places, that was the motherland, but of course I did not tell him that. I figured he would not talk to me anymore or worse, he would kick me out. He continued by saying the narrow road is the best because whenever I achieved my trip on this road, at the end of it, there would be great rewards, and that was Heaven. I was thinking, well, I am already there, and it was not that difficult to get here, the road was not narrow, and yes, it is sort of rewarding. He was the wisest man I have met, and to me, he was my second guarding angel after my grandmother.

Heaven was the first place that I had to cross the main street to gain access to its gates. It was not that far from Hell and Purgatory; the main street separated them. Sometimes when it rains, you cannot cross the main road because of the water that was running down at full speed. The current was so powerful it could drag a car all the way down to Stevenson's school. Whenever I went back to Purgatory while it was raining, I usually got stuck there. I would call my aunt and let her know I would not make it home and that would upset her because I was her responsibility, and she could not keep her eyes off of me. I could spend the whole day out of her sight, but when it came to nighttime, I had to be home, I had to be by her side. Being in Heaven changed everything. One thing in particular was the fact I had never set foot in Hell anymore, not that I have forgotten about it, I did not feel the need to go back, and over time, I would stop visiting Purgatory as well.

All three of us, Stevenson, Aunt Yaya, and I moved to Heaven that night, and I liked that neighborhood instantly. It was quiet and not too far from my school. We moved in with another family, a woman who my aunt used to take care of when she was a teenager alongside my cousin, but she left and started a family of her own. That would be the reason why we had to split the first floor in half. A wall separated both sides, and on my side there would be a gallery connected to the entrance door. The living room was connected to a hallway that led to Yaya's bedroom, and then the kitchen and the bathroom. In front of the bathroom door was another hallway that led directly to the main gate. My room was on the left side if you are heading to the main gate, and I had shared it with Stevenson for a short period. On the other side of the first floor there was the same thing except they had only one bedroom, and it was a huge one. That woman had two boys, and her husband was living with us as well, but most of the time he was out of the city working. That was the first time in my life I felt like I had a perfect family. It was awesome living in Heaven, and I had pretty much everything I ever wanted, everything I had ever dreamed of came true.

Heaven would be the place where I would have to say goodbye to Stevenson. This was the place where we had to go our separate ways, and God knows how much I wanted him to stay. I still did not tell him how sorry I was for those dark days I had caused him to endure. I still did not want him to forgive me. Some actions do not deserve forgiveness even if the victim is willing to forgive. I did not merit such remission, and this would be my cross to carry until the end of my time here on earth. There were some issues when we first got there in Heaven. As usual, my aunt always hired a maid to take care of the house because she was too old to take care of it by herself, and she could not take the heat when she was cooking, but she still used to cook me my favorite meal. The maid was supposed to take care of the whole first floor. It did not matter who was paying her; both sides used to be taken care of daily, but the woman with whom we shared the first floor seemed to have an issue with Stevenson, and she demanded he cleaned the whole house with the maid. That sounded absurd to me, and she also demanded he cleaned after her two sons.

I was enraged when Stevenson told me about the situation and what he had been doing. I decided to make the whole situation my own, and I stepped into Stevenson's shoes for the first time. It felt great to stand up for him like that, but at the same time I regretted doing so because it cost us our relationship. His mother had to come in and try to fix the issue, but the woman would not have him around without him doing all the work she insisted he does. Not too long after the conflict, Stevenson left us to go to *Delmas* to live with his older brother, and a few months from the date he left Heaven, he came back with his brother, except this time he moved back in our old home in Purgatory where his big brother would be in charge of everything.

That would be the most compelling reason behind the fact that I used to visit Purgatory daily, just because Stevenson was there, and I loved being around him. Almost every day after school you would find me there sitting on the back of an old car talking nonsense and telling dumb jokes with him. After all, Heaven was just as good as Purgatory was to me. Now with Stevenson gone, I had spent all my time alone, which was rewarding in a way. I had more time to think now and more time to focus on my writings. That was when I came up with the idea of writing a book about all the neighborhoods I have been living in and how they have shaped me into a better man.

My room turned into a human brain. That was where all my new thoughts as a full-grown man were born. I was seventeen when I moved into this new community, and according to my aunt and the landlord, I already had the mind of a wise man. Some would say I got weirder, mostly my classmates, because my view of the world had differed from theirs and the way I saw human beings had changed as well. I had developed a passion for human behavior and common sense. Even my aunt had sensed I was becoming a whole new person, and she had accepted me for the way I was and she had also given me my space to do so.

Sometimes when I was locked up in my room thinking and writing, the two brothers, the sons of that woman sharing the floor with us, would be outside my door waiting for me to let them in so they could play video games. That would be the reason why I let them take my Nintendo 64 outside and give me the chance to focus on my work. Those brothers were always fighting. They were kids, and that was what kids do. The older one was probably nine, and the younger one was around five. They were consistently fighting, and they would come to me to fix their issues. That was how Heaven had turned me into a judge. They would explain to me the reason behind the fights and would ask me to figure out who was guilty. I grew up listening to people saying all the time there were two sides to a story, and later in my life, I would learn there were three of them. During my time in Heaven, my mentality changed, and this theory did not make too much sense to me. I would sit there listening to their story, and then it got me to thinking: One of them knew the answer to their problem. Why did they need me to help them figure out who was guilty and who was innocent?

After listening to their stories for days, I realized there was only one side to a story, someone messed up. That was all. Someone was not right, and that led to chaos and trouble. Find that person, and the problem will be solved. The funny part was, only the two of them knew who messed up. I could not help them; I was not there to witness whatever happened between the two of them. The last time they got into a fight and came to me to figure out the whole situation, I told them to go back and talk to each other and figure out who was the one who started the entire mess. That seemed to help them, and since then, they stopped coming to me to solve their problems.

Another issue I seemed to have was how people around me acted and how they apologized. When it came to apologizing to someone, it does not mean the victim automatically has to forgive you. Most people seem to think once they apologized for some pain they have caused, they have earned that forgiveness, but that is not always the case. Most parents, especially in Haiti, would argue if someone recognizes they have done something wrong and that person apologized and took full responsibility for his action, then that person deserved forgiveness. I came to think that is the most insane way of forgiving someone, not that I do not want to forgive people. I will forgive you, but the thing is, does that person want to be forgiven? It is not up to me to forgive someone; I believe that it is up to them.

The way it works for me is bizarre, and I have been judged many times about this, but it is amazing how we tend to follow what we have heard from our ancestors. I will forgive, and I have done so, but the way I forgive is different from how most people do it. When someone is apologizing, he is giving the victim the option of accepting the apology or denying it, let's not forget about that. After apologizing to me, I would ask you a straightforward question, and me accepting your apology depends on how you answer that question. I would ask, "What happens if I do not forgive you?"

Most people apologizing to me would say it is whatever, and they did what they were supposed to do. They would claim they came clean and apologized, and if I did not forgive them that would be my problem. They would say it is not the end of the world if I did not accept their apology. Life goes on. To me, that would be the most meaningless apology ever. Why come to me in the first place if me not accepting your apology would not make you feel at least a little bit bad about yourself? Now, what is the point of me accepting such an apology? I think it is necessary to ask that simple question to one who is willing to apologize. If you not accepting their apology would hurt them, therefore, you have no choice but to forgive them.

I have lost quite some friends over this, and frankly, I believed it was worth it. Being in Heaven opened my eyes to a new reality; it has shown me how the world wants you to behave like a hypocrite. Everybody wishes for you to participate in all of their hypocritical activities. People tell you they do not like liars when they are the biggest ones. They do not want you to lie to them, but they do not realize they will never be ready to face the truth. They want to hear whatever it is they want to hear. They are too comfortable with how things are, how things have been, and they do not want to see change or try something new. If you are to try something new, you would be the beast, the enemy, the weird one.

We are always saying we are only human and we are not perfect. Maybe it is society itself that is keeping us from being perfect. Perhaps it is our minds that are keeping us from being so because we tend to follow more than being real to oneself. There is no need to prove anything to anyone. All that matters is being yourself, and that is how perfection comes into existence. We have made it quite difficult for one to be himself, and I am living proof. As a new resident of Heaven, I had to learn how to blend in with other people. I had to hide my true self for others to feel comfortable. If I at least tried to be myself, they would ask me who the hell I think I was, or they would tell me I do not belong here, and I need to go back to whatever planet I came from. One could be perfect, and I know there are plenty of them around, but do we allow them to be so? Being true to yourself, being real is all it takes to be the perfect one, and you have the power to do so within yourself.

Heaven had been a blessing, and it had taught me most of the life lessons. I never thought this would be the place where my worst nightmare would come to life; it was too sweet of a home for such an incident to happen. It had shown me so much, taught me so much, I did not think I needed schooling anymore. Up until this day, the most crucial lesson that place taught me still follows me around. It showed me the one person who makes another feel special or important is the one who is punished by the result of his good deeds. If you make me feel special, why would I mistreat you? You made me, and for that, I should worship you, not chase you around or beat you or even kill you no matter what the situation is. Be humble and always acknowledge how you came about.

I had also learned I could not be that cocky kid who wanted everybody to know he was around and always correcting others when they were wrong. That kid was long gone, and now I have learned to be quiet and listen. It is not always helpful to correct others. Listen and maybe you will learn something new. Before I knew it, such a nice neighborhood would show me something I would never be ready to accept; it would give me such an experience no matter how hard I have trained, I would never be prepared to face. Just like my grandmother Ana used to tell me, "Every good has its own evil shadow following it and at some point, when the time changes, it will catch up with it."

That was the case with Heaven. Heaven's evil caught up with her on that exact date: "Tuesday, January 12th, 2010."

CHAPTER SEVENTEEN

HEAVENLY, YET DISASTROUS

Both Hell and Purgatory were a thing of the past. Heaven was the only thing that mattered to me at that time, not that I forgot about the other neighborhoods, how could I? They have profoundly contributed to me being in Heaven; they have shaped me and paved the way for me to reach such a nice neighborhood. They were a thing of the past because I was not allowed to go back to my old ways. My mission was to keep pushing forward and keep on working very hard in the hope of improving myself. The temptation became stronger every day and was one step behind me, always trying to catch up to me, but Heaven was my shield. She was my sole protector. She reminded me every day how far I had come, and I should not give up now. It was time for progression, not regression. Just like my first love, I had fallen in love with Heaven at first sight, and it had become my second love. She had all my attention, and I devoted the rest of my life to her. I promised her she would always be the one to occupy my heart; she would be the one to inherit such a spirit she had given me. I had been faithful to her, I had completely stopped going back to Hell and Purgatory to prove my loyalty to her, and such an act might have shifted the way life was supposed to go for me.

Just like most relationships, sacrifices are essential. That is the key to maintaining a steady and healthy relationship. That was the glue that kept Heaven's and mine together for such a short time. This new neighborhood had become the only thing that could take my mind off Hell, but Hell would always be the root of my upbringing. Just like most Haitians would say, "This is the place where my parents buried my umbilical cord," meaning there is no way one would ever forget their home no matter where they end up in life. I did not forget about my friends. According to them, I was not their friends anymore, but to me, our friendship got a whole lot better than when we were hanging out back in the days. Not a single day went by without them popping in my head. The trips to the mountains, the Saturday mornings where we would cook together and head to the beach for swims and peaceful rests under the coconut trees. How could I forget the silly jokes, the fights, and the high-tension arguments we used to have? They were all memories. Those do not die, and they were the only things that mattered. Those days at the soccer fields where I would find true peace when madness was occupying my mind, how could I forget that? Those days under the wicked sun where a bunch of us would wait and hope someone would come in with a soccer ball so we could start playing and showing off our dribble moves. Those are unforgettable, but still, Heaven was the only thing that was in control of my heart when I moved there, nothing else.

Ever since I moved to Purgatory, my visits to Hell had started to slow down. I used to go there almost every day hoping to see my cousin and head back to the soccer field to spend the rest of the day. After my grandmother's passing, I just stopped going up until I moved to Heaven. When I finally went back after such a long time, it was like everything had changed and everybody I knew thought I was someone else. The residents of Hell could see I was physically changed. I was much taller, and I had the worst case of acne, which had been a struggle during my teenage years. They could see I was not the same person morally as well. They asked me lots of questions, some of which they did not want the real answers to, but I learned how to be around people and make them feel as comfortable as possible. Most people in Hell had seemed to like the new person I had become. A few did not. They thought I was faking it to get all the attention, but to be honest, I just wanted to get a taste of Hell after such a long absence. That one lady had told me to get on my knees so she could pray for me so I would never change and keep on making progress. That was when I came to the realization the old kid from Hell had passed, and a new one had been born after such a prayer was over.

It was a Monday morning, and I decided to skip school that day to go back and visit the old neighborhoods. I went through the Mariani marketplace just so I could avoid visiting Purgatory first. After talking to most of the residents of Hell who knew me as that troubled kid back then, I made my way to the old castle. I knocked on the door, and the lady from that family that was renting the first floor opened it for me. I greeted her and asked her if my cousin was home. That day was my lucky one, for she told me she was upstairs, probably sleeping. I saw the fifteen stairs, and I smiled, but they looked different now, they looked old and tired. I cautiously got up the stairs and looked around, for I had missed the house so much. I ended up on the first balcony; I made my way through the hallway and entered my cousin's room. She was sleeping like a baby. I did not wake her up, but I did head to the other balcony and gazed over the whole neighborhood. My head could almost touch the ceiling now, and I had to duck to look at what once was a soccer field. I felt at ease; I felt like I belonged there again, except for the fact *Heaven* was home, patiently waiting for my return.

As I was standing there, reminiscing about the old times, someone snuck up behind me and obscured my view with their hands. I tried to figure out who it was, but it was sort of hard to identify the individual, but the perfume smelled familiar. I was no genius, but I had to guess it was my cousin, given the fact she was the only one in the house that day besides the lovely family that was renting from her. I said her name, and still, the person kept their hands on my face. Now my head was rocking back and forth as my cousin was letting me know how much she had missed me. When she finally let go of my head, I turned around and hugged her as she was trying to push me away because she did not want me to meet her morning breath. She looked as different as everyone else I used to know back in the days, but her smile had never changed, and her cooking got a whole lot better. Everything had changed; even the sun smiled differently in Hell.

We talked for an extended period, and she had offered to cook me some food, which I happily accepted because I missed her super-hot meals. That was the last time I had to meet and talk to her, and it was worth it. I had no idea why I went back to Hell that day, but Heaven must have known I had to do it because that would be my last chance to get to see the loved ones from Hell. As we were conversing while eating, in the middle of the conversation, she asked me something that had nothing to do with what we were discussing.

"How is your girlfriend?" Dannie asked me with a weird smile on her face, and I dropped the fork with the pasta still wrapped around it on the table and started laughing.

We both laughed, and suddenly I stopped by asking her, "What girlfriend?"

I was not that close to my cousin; we were not that comfortable. To me, she was just a younger version of my Aunt Yaya. She did not play around, and she had never asked me that type of question before. That was when I had realized I was not a kid anymore; that was when I had realized I was ready to take on the challenges life had to offer.

I have spent the entire day in Hell, and it was one of the best days I had in my whole life. My next stop was the soccer field, but before I went there, I took a good look at it from the balcony, and it was not the same. Everything had changed, even that oak tree. It looked old and had lost some of its branches. The river stayed the same, and before I went to the soccer field, I made sure I baptized myself in there with some other guys who were trash talking in there. After the baptism, I headed straight to the soccer field, shirtless and all happy because I was about to check on my old friends. Some of them were eager to see me after so long, and most of them felt like I betrayed them and I was just a fake friend, for I stopped coming over and hang out. I knew they would not understand, for they were still in Hell hoping to find their Purgatory, and because of that I forgave them. The truth was, it felt great reaching out to the old folks in Hell, given the fact it was the last time they got to see me, and if I could go back and change that, I would have done it a lot more.

After such a beautiful day in Hell, the time had come for me to head back to Heaven. She was calling, for she was the most jealous person I had ever met. On my way back home, I met some more people with whom I used to spend some time with. One of them was Farah, the friend who caused the photo incident. She had grown into a fine woman, and she told me she had a kid now. I was shocked but happy for her because she used to say to me she hoped one day she would have a little one running around the house. She had completed that task, and I hugged her and laughed about the whole situation that happened between the two of us. I also met Stevenson on my way back, and he was almost as tall as me. As I was talking to Farah, he showed up from the river with his best mates.

When Farah and I were done talking, he showed up and said, "Farah! You are fine, girl! I would love to be the father of your second child." Then an evil laugh escaped his lips.

I slapped him on the shoulder and hugged him firmly as I said, "This is the Stevenson I had missed!"

We walked and talked our way to Purgatory.

We talked about stupid stuff and the ass-whooping his dad used to give us back in the days, but we ignored the fact I used to beat and treat him like he was not human. I knew in the back of his mind he was thinking about that because I was. If the aggressor was thinking about it, just imagine what the victim's brain looked like at that time. He grew up to be a fine young man, a bit wiser than he was before, but still kicking it with the ladies. Until this day, I do not know his secret. I do not know how he does it. I guess that is one secret he is willing to take to his grave. Lucky for me, I had my grandmother, and her secret on how to catch love was the only one I held on to in the hope to give my heart what it most desired. When we had reached Purgatory, I received the same welcome I had when I entered the gates of Hell; it was magical. It was great to see my old friends again and to tell them about how beautiful Heaven was, and she was the reason why I had stopped coming over and check on them, but deep down my heart, they were always present.

Most people I knew from Purgatory were gone. Some of them were dead, but most had had their own families and moved out to other neighborhoods in the hope of finding their own Heaven. As soon as I got there, I ran straight to Rambo's house. He was not that eager to see me because we saw each other every day at school, but his cousin, my best friend Jumel, was so excited to see me that it made me feel uncomfortable. We talked up until the day escaped, and right after that I went back into the old house where I had to face a lot of great memories. Stevenson's older brother was responsible for the house at that time. I did not have a good relationship with him, but we talked sometimes. I greeted him as I made my way past the gallery and headed straight to what was once my room a while ago. A lot of good memories came back to me as I entered that room. That was the place where I had held a gun for the first time, and this was the very same place where I found out I was a man. That was the place where I learned how to cope with some life challenges as well. That room would always play an essential role in my life.

The time came for me to leave for Heaven and, to be frank, I did not want to leave yet. I wished I could spend the night over there, but Heaven was calling. That was where I belonged now, that was where I was meant to be, that was the place that was created for me to endure the worst pain. It felt like part of me already knew this would be the last time I would get to see them, and I was not ready to go yet. When Heaven called, you could not ignore that. That was on call you do not wish to miss, and if you missed that call, you do not get a second one. It was about nine o'-clock when my foot left the house as I said my goodbyes to everyone who was inside. Stevenson walked me to the main street as we talked about family issues. I asked him to come to Heaven with me. Instead, he pushed me on the back as I crossed the street. My best guess was he was not ready to enter Heaven yet. He still had to find himself in Purgatory.

On the side of the road, I stood there for quite some time looking at him smiling and waving at me, and finally, he yelled out, "Just go, man, my hand freaking hurts already. Tell Auntie Yaya I said I love her."

For some reason, I felt the urge to cry, but I sucked it up because that was one thing you did not want to do in front of him. He would have made fun of me for the rest of my life.

I looked at him, I smiled proudly, and then I crossed my arms on my chest and told him we would see each other pretty soon. What I did not know was the fact "soon" never came. I believe he went back to his older brother's house in *Delmas* the following morning because after the big event I did not see him for the rest of the days I was allowed to spend in Heaven. I went home that night, and this was the first time I felt how strong loneliness could get. I had been alone the entire time there ever since Stevenson had left, but this sort of loneliness was different. I was lonely to the point where I needed some attention. I needed to go back to Hell and Purgatory and have another blast with the loved ones, but that was not the case. I spent that night thinking about moving back to Hell with my cousin and wondered how things could have been if we did not move from Purgatory. I do not know how I did it, but I fell asleep with my head on my aunt's lap as she was telling me stories about her childhood. She woke me up and told me to go to my room and rest. I went in there, slammed my whole body on the bed, and that was the best sleep I have ever had.

◆ ◆ ◆

I passed all the tests that were given to me by the previous neighborhoods, and now the time came for me to take the final exam. I had been a good student, took all my notes and studied hard to ace the final exam, but I did not study hard enough because a big fail awaited me. That morning, Tuesday of course, when I woke up, I had no idea my life would take a considerable turn ten hours later. That morning was like all the other ones. I got up around six to the sweet sound of Ansy Derose playing on the little green radio my mother had sent me. The smell of sautéed greens and onions and some other Haitian spices said their good morning to me as they waited for the egg to join them. I did the usual; I joined my aunt in her morning prayer. I did not pray; I let her do the praying. I knelt right next to her and listened to her demands and thanks to God. Right after that, I headed outside and felt the morning breeze go through my tank top and let the morning sun rest a little bit on my face. After having my sweet time with nature, I headed back inside to have my breakfast, Haitian-style scrambled egg with buttered bread and a glass of freshly squeezed grape-fruit juice. To me, that was the best way to start the day, with "*Merci*" by Ansy Derose playing low in my room...I just wished the day would end the same way it started.

I then proceeded to get some water from the well so I could take my morning showers, which were interrupted by the brothers kicking at the door and yelling, "Your time is UP!"

After showering, I headed back to my room where Ansy Derose was still playing, except this time my favorite song was on. "*Fanm Peyim*"

(My country's women) was playing, and every time I heard that song, it reminded me of my first love, and that morning, she was part of my thoughts. It was a song about how beautiful our women are and how lucky we Haitian men are to have them by our side. That song went on by describing them mostly about their natural beauty, which very much reminded me of the best times I used to have back in Hell. This morning might have been the best one I had in my life, and I did not think it was possible for me to have one exactly like that again. I would do anything to experience such a morning again, but the evening of that day I would not wish to experience ever again in my life. All set and ready to go, I left the house and headed straight to the place I hated the most, school.

Tuesday, that was my favorite day of the week when I was living in Haiti. Why was it my favorite day? Just because after school, I would come home and expect to have my favorite meal *"Du riz Jardinier"* which means "gardener's rice." It was a dish where rice was the main ingredient, then red beats, kale, onions, red peppers, crab, some other Haitian spices, and anything edible you could find in a gardener's crop. Just because of that, my love for Tuesdays grew exponentially. All my life, all my Tuesdays had been great, never complained about a single one, but this Tuesday was way different. That Tuesday would always stay on my mind until the end of time. I found it a bit ironic how Heaven had chosen my favorite day to give me my final test. That was how I knew she was not playing around.

Everything seemed odd that day. On my way to school I saw the kid I usually gave a dollar. He stopped me and goes, "Do you have money to eat during *rekreyasyon* (lunch break)?"

I said, "Yes, I always do, and as a matter of fact, today's your lucky day. Those ten bucks are for you."

As I handed him the money, he had a crazy smile that I found so lovely, and he gently pushed my hand away with the money. That was the first time Zach had refused cash from me. Not only did he refuse, but he also reached into his pocket and gave me five and insisted I take it and put it inside my shoes, and so I did. That was strange, but I kept on going my way without questioning him about what he just did. The school was not too far away from *Heaven*. It was probably seven minutes away from the house, and when I was on my way there I could not shake the thought of me walking back home from school so I could enjoy the food that was waiting for me back there. For me, on Tuesdays, I did not go to school. I just went there to kill time then go back home to enjoy my favorite meal. I would sit in class and not really paying attention to what the professor was talking about, and sometimes I would go outside and hang out with the other students who were skipping class.

When I got to the school, some of the teachers were not there, and that was unusual. We had some free periods for ourselves. It felt like God's last supper; we were eating, telling jokes and waiting for the worst to happen. I never had that much fun in school. That school was the worst place I ever attended. From kindergarten to eleventh grade, I had been going to the same school, and I have to tell you that day was the best one I had in there. This Tuesday was odd, but excellent. For the first time, I felt like I belonged in this school. I was a victim of bullying pretty much every day. If anybody had a joke to make, all they had to do was take a quick look at me, and there it was, the perfect joke ever. I was not too fond of school, not because of all the works and studies, but because of the bullying, and I had to thank my bullies. Because of their actions, I learned how to take a joke and how to prevent others like me from getting bullied.

We were having so much fun that day we did not even realize how fast the time went by. When the bell rang for us to leave the school, I did not know I had lost my ten dollars, the ones I wanted to give Zachary. I usually saved my lunch money so I could buy some *Fresko* and drink it on my way home with some chicken patties. Now that my ten dollars was gone, my walk home would be a bit sad. Then I remembered Zach gave me those five bucks, and that had made my walk home a bit sweeter. When I finally got home, things were different. My aunt was not there for my after-school hug, and there was no "*Du riz jardinier!*" Now imagine a dog that's been waiting for you to throw him your chicken bone; instead, you ate it while he was watching you do so. I was as mad as that dog that day. Instead, there was cornmeal with some chicken sauce and mango juice.

I did not even touch the food, for I was upset and a bit vexed. I went straight to my room without asking about my aunt's whereabouts. I didn't even take my uniform off, just spent about three minutes talking to myself in the mirror then hopped on the bed and slept a great deal. My sleep was then disturbed by a thunderous noise. Then another noise followed, and that one sounded like a choir performing a classic song, like a bunch of people crying at the same time, and it pierced through my soul. As I woke up from my long nap, I could feel the ground shaking. I immediately thought it was a tractor or some other type of heavy-duty equipment making their way past the neighborhood. I got up and made my way outside, as the ground was still shaking. I could not believe what I saw. That was the moment where I wish I were blind.

My mind traveled back in time as I pictured the beautiful moments I had back then. I saw my grandma standing halfway through those fifteen stairs. I saw the beach and my mates having a swimming contest, and then I saw my first love, the first day I saw her in front of that store buying some cooking goods. I saw that smile again for the second time; we got lost into each other's eyes again. I saw my godfather running toward me with a handful of mangoes screaming my name, "Jenkins! Jenkins!"

Right then and there, I snapped right out of my zone as he was yelling out my name while blending in with the dust that was showering the whole neighborhood.

CHAPTER EIGHTEEN

HEAVEN'S WRATH (EVIL TUESDAY)

Just like the "*Bois Caiman*" ceremony, that Tuesday nature participated in that final exam I had been preparing for since my second birth. We have a saying in Haiti that goes, "*Bel fanm se male*," which translates, "Beautiful women are trouble." I never thought of that saying up until this Tuesday afternoon. All that mattered to me was the fact Heaven was beautiful, but I did not take my time to analyze what could go wrong in there. I did not even consider the possibility things could go wrong. I thought to myself this is Heaven! It is all fun and perfect, but what I did not know was the fact that behind such a beauty, the worst day of my life was hiding. That proverb, my whole life, I found it to be a bit barbaric. I could not shake the thought that something that beautiful could have an evil side to it. To me, everything beautiful was perfect. I started questioning that when my grandmother told me about everything great had its own evil shadow following it.

The timing was right for Heaven, and her own evil shadow caught up with her. It was almost five in the afternoon when I woke up from such a vibration coming from my room's floor. I got up from the bed and made my way outside as I tried to keep my balance. As I opened the front door, I could not understand what was going on. First, I looked up to the sky; it was not blue anymore. It looked angry, and it was a bit gray due to the vast amount of dust that was flying over the neighborhood. The mountains were invisible for a while. I could not see any of the green pastures and the tall coconut trees, and that was when I had realized Heaven was showing me her evil side. When my dead godfather screamed out my name, I woke up from zoning out and faced reality. My entire life, I never knew I would be able to witness such terror. I never knew a solution of blood and dirt, mostly dirt, was possible.

I could not believe my eyes. At that moment, I thought I was in a horrible dream, and I was hoping to wake up from it, but it was far from being a dream. That was the real deal, that was Heaven's way of teaching me what it meant to be a human being. That was her way of showing me the reason why I was sent to be here with her. As I walked down the dusty street, I met the saddest faces ever. I saw people crying with dirt on their faces, bloody faces, and even people who seemed to not even care about what had hit us that day. It was like when my godfather and grandmother died, except this time, it was a million times worse. It was more like my grandmother and my godfather's death combined to the millionth power, and it was a gruesome scene for anybody to witness. I walked, and at some point ran without even knowing where I was going. I guess one could say I was in shock. All I remember was I needed to find Aunt Yaya, and I had better find her alive. At that moment, nothing was on my mind but my aunt. I felt guilty of being mad at her for not cooking my favorite food that day, and now I could not even find her to tell her or even show her how sorry I was. She had to be alive, and I would not rest until I had found her.

I kept on moving and kept my eyes almost everywhere in the hope of finding my aunt. When I passed Zach's house, it was no longer standing, it looked like a bombing site, and his home had later become his tomb. After walking for so long with no sight of my aunt, I made my way back home and tried to wrap my mind around all the pain I had seen that day. The way back was worse, I saw a great deal of blood, blood everywhere, people with blood on their faces, body parts and debris from col-lapsed homes, dead bodies almost everywhere. I could hear people under collapsed houses screaming for help and the sudden silence that came as life abandoned them. Sadness hit me hard that day, up until I saw my aunt back home, waiting for me to come to her without a scratch on me. She went to the market to buy the ingredients to make my favorite dish, but she was lucky because on her way back to the house she made a quick stop to her church when the earthquake hit.

As soon as my eyes met hers, I felt relieved, and I have felt alive again. It was the same feeling as if I was walking in the desert for days and I have finally found some water. I hugged Yaya to the point where if it were possible, we would have become one person. We were all standing outside of the house just hearing the cry of a nation in peril. I told Yaya how sorry I was for being that mad at her earlier about not having my food on time, and I was counting on that food. It did not seem to be a problem for her because she told me she did not even know I was mad. In a way, I earned her forgiveness. Most people in Heaven was safe, but those in the heart of the capital, most of them who lived not too far from the church where I received my first communion (Paroisse St. Charles) were not. We were not allowed to go back inside our home. We were to spend the whole night outside comforting some of the neighbors who were wondering where their loved ones could be at this very moment. Our landlord's wife was one of those people. I remember her crying and panicking because of her son, possibly the only friend I had in Heaven. He went to his school, and he was not back home on time.

We were all waiting up until ten at night in the hope of seeing him, but he never showed up. We were all sitting and comforting the landlord's wife. The landlord was a strong man, and he believed throughout the night his son was fine and he would be there soon. There were prayers and chants all night, but you could still hear the cry of the people. Finally around eleven he showed up, and it was like the sky had opened up and

God had descended and handed him over to his mother. I had never seen such love since my grandmother's passing, and the way his mother hugged and kissed him took me back to the best times I had with my beloved grandmother. I was a bit jealous; I decided to join in and hugged them as well, and I was more than welcome to do so. Polo, that was the nickname I had given him. He was a bit dusty, and I could tell he went through a lot because his faculty was in the heart of the capitol. After all the hugs and kisses, he sat down and went on about all the things he had seen and said we were lucky we were not living in the middle of the capital city because there was nothing left of it. Mostly everything was destroyed, and traffic was the reason behind his tardiness.

One of the families that was living in the neighborhood was related to our landlord, and thanks to them we were able to use their large backyard to take our showers. They, too, had a well, and I took responsibility to get water to whoever needed it, just like I was in charge of doing so in the house. After Polo shared with us how his day went, he ran to the backyard in the hope of getting water and taking a nice shower, but that was a bit impossible for him to do. He was still in shock, and I could not imagine the things he had seen considering what I have seen on my journey to find Aunt Yaya. I walked him to the backyard in the dark and kept on talking to him to make sure he was fine. When we reached the well, he tried to pull up the bucket of water from it, but that seemed to be a bit challenging for him because he was shaking. I offered to help and get him the bucket of water, and as soon as he was about to get ready to shower, my aunt came rushing in and told him not to do so. In Haiti, we believe whenever someone is in shock, they should not be showering, especially with cold water. That could lead to severe illness and possibly death.

I remember feeling the urge to go back to Hell and Purgatory that night to check on the loved ones, but I was not allowed to go there. My aunt would not let her eyes off of me because she did not want me to fall victim of the aftershocks. She wanted me to be by her side all day and night because I was her responsibility. I could have gone to Hell and Purgatory on my quest to find her, but that was not on my mind at that time. I just wanted to see her and make sure she was okay. I could not bear losing another one close to me after I lost my grandmother. I started to feel what it was like to be human. I began to know what it felt like to lose someone you deeply loved. That was just the beginning; the worst was yet to come. After the 7.0 magnitude earthquake hit us, small ones kept on happening now and then. It was not over, and that would be the reason behind us not being able to go back inside our home, and also the reason why I was forbidden to go back to the previous neighborhoods.

The next day, around two in the morning, when we finally had a little time to ourselves to sleep, we woke up to some people screaming water was coming. I could not make out the difference between reality and a dream. I thought maybe I was finally dreaming based on the fact that I did not have enough sleep the previous day. Perhaps I imagined things or I was hallucinating, but it felt as real as the whole earthquake was. The entire neighborhood was running for their lives. They were looking to reach high ground to beat the tsunami that was on its way to give Heaven her perfect bath. The thing was, when everyone was running for their lives, my aunt could not do the same, and she had told me that it was okay for me to join the others. That was another tough decision I had to make. I could not leave behind the only woman who had cared for me for years, and I certainly could not carry her to where I was supposed to go, but I chose to stay back with her. There was no better way to die. Dying with the person you cared about the most seemed like a logical thing to do at that moment, so my choice was made. She did not agree with it, and I did not need her approval. I decided, and that was final. Some people in the neighborhood knew it was a scam so some people could steal some of our stuff while we were trying to save our lives. My aunt and I stayed behind with a couple of people, and we were waiting to meet our maker. There is nothing worse than knowing how you are going to die and to

know exactly how it is going to happen. I could not bear leaving her behind and losing another part of my soul. I sat beside her on the floor as
she hummed some gospel songs and waited for the worst to happen. If
that were a dream, I would hope nobody had to wake me up.

◆　◆　◆

After that incident, I spent most of my days in Heaven with my aunt, and
she kept her eyes on me all the time. I could not go anywhere, and the
level of boredom was off the chart. I had to come up with ideas to have
a little bit of fun in the neighborhood, but that was not too successful. I
just did what I used to do in a daily basis before the earthquake. I took a
pen and a piece of paper and started writing poetry and short stories, some
of which I would tell my aunt to get some smiles out of her. On the third
day after the earthquake happened, my best friend from Hell came to visit
us. I tried not to talk about him too much because I did not want people
to interfere with what we had going. People tend not to like seeing people
having a good connection. He did have some good news; he was alive,
then he gave us the bad news. He told us about how the people from Hell
and Purgatory were holding up. I was shocked when he had told me how
Hell was destroyed by the event.

I got paralyzed when I realized that the castle in which I grew up was no longer standing.

"Only the garage door is standing. Everything else collapsed with your
cousin in it, but she managed to survive," he told me.

At that point nothing could stop me from traveling back to Hell, but
I had to respect my aunt's commands. That was the only person I was not

allowed to disobey. I was not allowed to go back to the place that had everything to do with my existence, and that was the biggest regret I had. I would do anything to help out the residents of Hell, but it was not safe over there. Nothing was safe at that point in my life, not even us in Heaven. He then proceeded by telling us part of the house in Purgatory had some real damage, but it was not that bad. That was when I realized everything happened for a reason, and I had been following my aunt since day one for a reason. There was no doubt I would be dead if I stayed back with my cousin in Hell. I knew for a fact I would be in the house at that time, and it would have collapsed with me in it. The same thing goes for Purgatory because part of the ceiling in my room had fallen off. After the visit, my best friend had left us, and that was the last time I had seen him as well. On the third day, I decided to do something other than sitting there and write all day. I decided to go to the nearest hospital with Polo to visit his girlfriend's dad who was seriously injured during the event. I was surprised by the fact my aunt let me go with him and his cousin. She made sure Polo did not let me go to Hell or Purgatory and he was a man of his word. In a sense, he was tougher than Auntie Yaya that day. We walked for miles, and when we finally got there, I just wished we never set foot inside that hospital.

Polo's cousin was a hilarious man. On our way to the hospital, he kept telling us jokes, amusing ones in the hope of keeping our mind off the things we had seen on our way there. We stopped to drink some water from a fountain that was next to a collapsed house.

As we were drinking the water, he blurted out, "That water could be bad. It could be flowing through a dead body as we are drinking it."

I remembered Polo spitting The rest of the water straight to his face as his cousin was dying laughing. He had a dark sense of humor, but I still think he was a funny guy. He then took his boots off, and his feet looked extremely painful. I remember we were walking for miles, and as soon as he took his boots off, we busted out laughing because his feet were all about bumps and bruises, and it got swollen to the point where it looked like it was about to pop. He proceeded by making a song about his feet being like that and how the boots were the reason behind such a situation.

As soon as we set foot inside the hospital, my heart stopped, and I realized how lucky I was by watching such suffering and the state of the hospital. We were not allowed inside the hospital because of the after-shocks. All the patients were lying down on the hospital yard, most of them resting on the floor of the parking lot. It was the cruelest scene I had ever seen in my entire life. I saw all sorts of injuries as I walked among the helpless patients on the floor. At that point, I was not paying attention to Polo or anything he had to say; I did not even know he ex-isted. I got lost into the patients' worlds. For the first time in my life, I felt sympathy for my brothers and sisters. I was confused, for I did not know what was happening to me.

As I was rushing through to help a little boy who was in pain because he had lost his right arm, Polo had grabbed me and said, "Let the doctors do their job. He will be fine."

I pulled myself from him and rushed outside where I cried for a great deal. As I was out there crying, I remembered what Mrs. Virgine had said to me that day about crying.

"Look young one; there will be times when you will need those tears. They might come out, they might not. Fact is, you must let those feelings out however form they show up. Do not be ashamed of crying. That's just a taste of how life gets, and trust me young one, it will get harder."

I realized how right she was from witnessing such a scene. Life did get a whole lot harder for me to handle.

Polo's cousin came out to get me as he was trying to wipe my tears, but I did not let him do so. I was not trying to be disrespectful. I did not want him to cause my acne to be worse than it was back then given the fact he was touching his hideous feet earlier. I made my way back inside the parking lot and walked by a "*kamyonet*" (little bus) with a guy lying face flat on its bench. I spotted him on the corner of my eyes, and it seemed like he was wearing a red t-shirt, and he had dirt all over his face. I later realized this guy had no shirt on, and he was severely injured and he was lying there probably dead. No one seemed to care about him. I went ahead and greeted Polo's girlfriend's father who appeared to be doing fine for someone who was severely injured. He had that smile on his face, and he kept on saying God had saved his life, and he couldn't be happier. I could see the pain in his face, but he was good at hiding it as he was praising God through it. That man could not pee, and that had caused his lower abdomen to bloat. He had been rescued under debris when the event happened as he was reading the Holy Scriptures in his home.

As I stood there listening to him, other souls were departing the parking lot. I saw plenty of cadavers being transferred to some private morgue since the hospital morgue could not take any more bodies. When I saw this I thought to myself, *If God saved this guy, why didn't he save the other ones? Why didn't he prevent that kid from losing his right arm?*

Just like my aunt used to say, the Lord works in mysterious ways, but that day the Lord would have some serious questions to answer.

After such a long day at the hospital, we made our way back to Heaven. It was around two in the afternoon when my aunt was patiently waiting for my arrival. We did not have any phone signal at the time. If we had, she would probably have blown up Polo's phone to make sure I was okay. When we got back home, we were exhausted, but we did not have time to rest. We took a shower, and I had asked my aunt if I could go to Polo's church with him and his mother. Once again, she agreed. I had some personal questions to ask God about the whole situation. I was not a firm believer, but I did believe in God, not the one everybody else worshiped. I believed in a fairer God, I believed in a God who does not exist. I had some questions for the God the guy we visited was worshiping, and I needed some clarity on the whole situation.

At this point in my life, I started questioning myself. Out of all people, why was I spared? Why wasn't I suffering with the other ones? I was
not good enough. I was just that lousy kid from Hell who knew no better.
I used to cuss people out, fight other kids, and burn things. I was a ma-
nipulative guy, and I would do anything for everything to go my way. If
it was not my way, then it did not matter. Why them and not me? I was
an abuser, a liar, and a master manipulator. Why was I spared? That question remains a mystery until this day, and I do not think I will ever find
the answer to it. That was the same question I decided to ask God, the
one who everybody worships. I went to the church, it was a seventh-day
Adventist church, and it was no different from the one my aunt used to
attend. They had the same style of praising God, and the atmosphere was
all the same.

We made our way inside the church. Polo's mother was a member
of the church's council, so she sat up front. Polo and I sat in the back. As
the service began, we were asked to get on our knees and pray because
the end was near. I had been hearing that since I was a kid, but the end
never showed up. I did as the preacher instructed, and I just asked God,
Why did you spare me? over and over again. I just kept asking him in my
heart as the service continued, and I believe He got tired of my annoying
self and decided to hit us with another quake. I called that one the first
one's brother, for it was a bit strong.

That was the closest answer I had ever gotten to that question. Not a
fun way to get the answer to questions you have long waited to ask. It
was sort of ironic how that quake happened when the preacher was
preaching about not being scared. He was the first one to leave the church
to save his life. That would be one of the reasons why I do not go to
church unless someone invites me. I cannot be in a place where the leader
is more afraid than I am. To me, that makes no sense. I stayed inside with
Polo because my aunt always told me there was no safer place on this
planet than the house of God. I stayed in, not because I believed that to

be true 100 percent, but because at that point I had given up. Nothing else made sense to me anymore. The cathedral that was in the heart of the city was gone, but the crosses were intact. That was one of the houses of God, but still, it was destroyed by the event. I had given up, but later on I would have a great idea which would make me feel like a whole new person.

◆　◆　◆

After the service, I went back to Heaven and explained to my aunt what had happened, and she had a blast. She laughed so hard tears were dripping down her cheeks. The next day she decided to go to church and leave me in the neighborhood with the others. She trusted me enough to leave me by myself and know for a fact I was not going to go back to Hell or Purgatory. That idea had not crossed my mind at that moment, but I had a new plan, and it was the only thing that mattered to me that day. Before she left, she had given me some money to go to the nearest cybercafé and try to call my mother and let her know we are fine, but I did not do such thing. I used the money to pay the bus and head back to the hospital in the hope of volunteering to help in any way I could. I could not even believe I was about to do this. That was not who I was. I was not the helping type; I was not the one to make a situation better. I usually made situations worse and tried to profit from them.

As I was on the bus, I kept thinking to myself, *I am going to do this, and I cannot wait to do so.*

For the first time, I was excited to help out, I was happy to make my fellow Haitians, my brothers and sisters, feel better.

When I got there, there were fewer people than my first visit, and I already figured out what had happened to them. Patients were still lying down on the parking lot waiting to be taken care of by the only pair of doctors they had. As I was walking by them, I made sure some of them were comfortable. I fixed their blankets and even used the spare T-shirts I had in my backpack to make pillows for them. When I finally reach the front door of the hospital's office, I spotted a nurse, and I told her I was here to help and she could use me to do anything as long as I was helping. She was not very helpful, and she told me she was not in charge and I needed to talk to a doctor to do what I wanted to do. I did as she instructed, and hopefully I had found a doctor, a friendly one. I thought he might be a bit too young to be a doctor, but he was very understanding. I told him about my mission, and he believed it was a great idea given the fact they were shorthanded, but the other doctor, the older one, would not let me help. He asked me who sent me, was it another doctor, do I have a letter, and a bunch of other questions. I was heartbroken as I was leaving the hospital. My soul got crushed, and so did my heart. I stuck around, talked to a few patients, and listened to their stories, and got to know a bit about them. It was not much, but that was all I could do at that moment. I was a friend; I was a family member to the ones who had no one. I found myself surrounded by family members I never knew I had. They would share their food with me and tell me about themselves. That was all I ever wanted, and I got it just by helping the ones in need by reading them stories I wrote and having friendly conversations.

I did not know this would be my last night in Heaven when I got back from the hospital. My aunt was waiting for me, and she assumed I went back to Hell. I had to explain myself, and I did not know how to lie to my aunt with a straight face, so I had no choice but to tell her the truth.

She hugged me firmly then whispered slowly in my ear, "I am very proud of you, Roro."

I was confused as I said to her, "You are not mad?"

She then said she had no reason to be. She said I was out there for the people just like I was there for her when we heard a tsunami was on its way. That was when I realized I was for the people, and I could never be a politician in my country because by being one you had to forget about the people's need. We slept in cars after the whole catastrophe, and that night I could not sleep. I kept thinking about the patients I had seen, and all the dead bodies as well. Those people, they meant something to someone, they were a godfather, a Jean, an Ana to someone and now they were gone. The ones who had lost them had been feeling the same way I felt when I lost my grandmother. All the ones who survived the earthquake, they claimed to be survivors, but deep down they were all dead considering what they had lost. A house you could get back, a car, you could get that back as well, but your loved one, a heart that felt for you, that cannot be replaced. You cannot buy such a thing.

The most important thing I learned from that event was the fact it does not matter if you are rich or poor. When nature is angry, everybody pays the same price. We will all share the same room, which for me was that hospital's parking lot. There was not a particular room or some people getting better care than others because of the amount of money they had. There was no such thing. Everybody was in the same place, sharing the same floor and telling the same story: *They have survived.*

The only thing that truly mattered was the fact you need to be humble and accept one another as we are. Nothing beats acceptance to me, not even love. Take me for who I am then I will show you how perfect I am. Otherwise, you will always think you are better than me, and that will keep you from seeing my true self. To me, that is all it is about, be humble, be wise, and accept one another. That was the lesson *Heaven* had thought me. That was how I had been so different and so weird to some people I have encountered.

From Hell to Heaven, the journey had been the toughest, but still, I have to find my second Heaven. You will always have to better yourself. It is a long process, and it does not stop until you are out of the game. There will always be room for improvement no matter how good you think you are. Saturday, January 16th, 2010: That was the date when I had to kiss Heaven goodbye. I never imagined leaving Aunt Yaya's side, but her mission was over, and it was time for me to let go of her loving arms. I did not want to go, but I had to follow her orders and to disobey her was not an option. That Saturday morning, I woke up in the car with five dollars in my pocket. My aunt had put them there for me to go back to the cybercafe to give my mother a call. I did as she instructed, and sadly, the call went through. The worst thing was the fact my aunt was also there with me. If she were not, I would have lied about what my mother had told me to do. My mother had ordered me to pack my things and go to Delmas. I was told to pick up my little sister and head to the airport so we could come to the U.S. My mother had already talked to my aunt and told her it was time for me to go back to my first home, Boston, Massachusetts. I did not want to, but I had no choice. For the first time after the event, she went inside to pick what I was supposed to wear. I went in there with her because at the time I felt like dying in there with her would be better than leaving her behind like this. While we were in there with silence surrounding us, I was hoping another quake would hit, but thanks to her God, we had protection.

◆　◆　◆

There was no life without my aunt by my side, and I knew I would have to die and be born again for the third time in another country. I would have to go through the same process again. I would have to find a new Hell, Purgatory, and Heaven in that new country. She handed me a long-sleeved red shirt she had bought me years ago and a pair of gray pants with the new pair of shoes she had bought me for the upcoming exam (*Bac 1*) I was supposed to take. She gave me a bath and dressed me up like she used to when I was a kid and took me outside where we would say our goodbyes. When we stepped out of the house, it was like the earthquake had happened again. It was like January 12 all over again. My life had taken a considerable turn for the worse; I was not ready for such a chapter in my life. I had to look at my aunt in the eye as I was leaving her behind, and the worst part was I could not decide, I was not allowed to. My time in such a beautiful island was over. My happy hours were over, and now the time had come for me to take it to the next level. I was not ready to take on the next challenge, and I still needed my aunt's guidance to light my way so I could reach my destination. My aunt asked our landlord to take me to Delmas because she did not want to go there and go back to Heaven without me. As I was leaving, she called my name. I hoped she was going to say I could stay. Instead, she blurted out those three words, not that she loved me, but, *"Be yourself, son,"* as her cold palms held my face.

I confusedly smiled as she smiled back, and that smile was the last one I enjoyed before I left the country.

"Be yourself."

I was baffled, for I did not understand what she meant by that. At that time, I did not even know who I was; I was still figuring that out. One minute I was that crazy kid, and the next, all I wanted to do was help my fellow Haitians. Who was I? Was that for show or was that the way I truly felt inside? During the ride to Delmas, I kept thinking about that, and that sentence kept running in my head ever since, *Be yourself, son.* I tried to make sense of it ever since, and the only way it makes perfect sense is if I applied it to everyone else because there is no better world than the one within it contains people who are genuinely themselves and accept each other as they are. Accept everybody based on their perfection. Once again, you can be perfect; you only have to be the way you were born to be, the way you feel like you are supposed to be. You do not have to live for anybody else, you do not have to impress anyone, just be yourself. One thing is important to know, it is the fact there will be consequences to face for being yourself. That will not be an issue because once you have accepted yourself, you will be able to face anything that comes your way.

That ride to Delmas was gruesome because that was the first time I had taken my time to see how bad the earthquake destroyed the city—not only the sight, but the smell as well. Death was still lurking around even though it had been a few days since evil Tuesday. When I finally reached my destination, the landlord said his goodbyes and told me to never forget how I came about and to keep on fighting the good fight. He reminded me once again to take the narrow route, not the wide one, and I assured him that I would. I delivered the message that my mother had ordered me to deliver, and the three of us, my little sister, her godmother (Mrs. Pedro), and I left the neighborhood I resided in for a couple of days when I first came in Haiti to the States. We had to stay in the American embassy for a couple of days before we could leave the country due to some paperwork. From fifteen flights of stairs to a final exam from Heaven, the journey had been a tough one; the quest to become a better person had been a real one. Now, the time had come for me to be born again for the third time, and this time it began in New York.

BONUS

We all have our cross to carry; it depends on how courageous and how strong we are to acknowledge our wrongdoings to reach our destination while that cross is on our back. The weight of your cross depends on you knowing the things you are not too proud of, and the more you ignore it, the heavier the cross gets. To me, that is what pushes a man to improve and become a better one. With that being said, I do not think it is possible a person can change entirely. You can become a whole new person, whether good or bad, but you will still inherit your old ways. There is a Haitian proverb that goes, *"Mwen vann zoutim, men'm pa bliye metye'm."* That proverb is saying even though you sell all of your tools, you will never be able to forget how to get the job done. To me, change is the selling of your devices, the sale of your old habits, but how to practice the old habits is still going to be a part of that new and improved person you have become. There is nothing wrong with that, but the most important thing about change is how temptation-resistant you are.

One thing I am pretty sure of is the fact that hard times are signs a brighter future is on its way. Take it from me, I have been through Hell, but that was not the end for me. Just because you are in Hell does not mean you are doomed to stay there. Things will get better. If you got locked in there, you are yet to find the key and make your way to Purgatory. I once got locked up in Hell, and trust me, I wanted to stay in there, for it was fun and full of joy. I have found my way out and head toward what was going to be my liberation from my old habits and the search for a more empathetic type of self.

The point is, no matter how hard the situation gets, you are yet to make it to Heaven and liberate yourself. I came to the understanding that all the difficult times you are enduring are just the preparation of what is to come. We are not doomed to be the dark person we are, and there is always room for improvement. No matter what happened to you, no matter what society throws at you, keep on focusing on yourself. Keep on improving yourself. Accept yourself for who you are, and that way you will also be able to accept others no matter what their choices or beliefs are. With that being said, I have one last story to share with you, an experience I learned so much from when I was a resident of Hell.

THE DOG WHISPERER

Growing up, I was not allowed to have pets. Not because my aunt said so, but because she thought I was not responsible enough to take care of one. I hate to say it, but she was wrong. My first pet was our neighbor's, Joel. That was the first time I saw a dog so humble in my life. Her name was "Dola," meaning "dollar." She had white and yellow fur, and she was not a mad dog unlike the one that hated my guts, *Chwaziras*. I used to go to Joel's house every morning to give Dola some of my breakfast. I would also do so when we are having dinner. Over time, Dola and I developed a special bond; we became what you would call best friends.

She would follow me everywhere I went, even when I was going to school. She'd follow me there, and when it was time for me to enter the school's gates, her sad eyes would not allow me to do so. Every time she gave me the sad eyes, I had to be five minutes late, given the fact I have to buy her a hotdog and pet her for a few minutes and tell her to go back. Sometimes, she would wait the whole time outside the school to walk me back home. She was such a good friend. Sometimes, I had to wake up at four in the morning to avoid her so she wouldn't follow me to school because I could not afford to be late too much for classes. That did not stop her from coming to get me after school. She was what you would call a guardian angel. She was always there during the good and the bad times.

In Haiti, most people do not care about dogs. Some people beat them to death or abuse them just for fun. I used to get into many fights in my neighborhood defending dogs, even get my ass kicked once for Chwaziras, the dog that hated my guts. That one kid, Emilio, for some reason, decided to kick Chawziras in the face just because he felt like it. I could not stand there and watch this. Something had to be done about that. I quickly ran downstairs, went through the garage door, and pushed him. It was a coward move because Emilio was not expecting me to do that. He fell on his face as I pushed him on his back. Emilio was ten times bigger than me, so I don't have to go through all the details about that fight. I had a great ass-whooping as Chwaziras was watching. He was probably enjoying that moment because he had that look on his face every time a punch landed on my face.

After the beating, I was sitting on the side of the street, outside of my house where everybody was staring at the stupid kid who just got beat because of a silly dog. I did not see it that way, and I wanted the madness to stop. The way dogs were being treated in my neighborhood, I wanted to put an end to it. As my face was hurting, Dola came to me. She was on her way home, and as soon as she spotted me, she stopped as she realized something was wrong with me. I shut my eyes for a minute then opened them again, and she was right in front of my face. She gave me a few licks then proceeded to sit right next to me. I went back inside, washed my face, then had dinner with her as Yaya told me to get her out.

After that day, I became the dogs' God. I did not know what Dola did. She must have told every single dog in the whole neighborhood about what had happened. Now, not only Dola walked me to school, but Benji and Lito also joined in. Now I had to buy extra hotdogs for extra protection. Just like that, I became the dog whisperer. I had all the dogs in the palm of my hand, except for Chwaziras. Like Shakespeare said in sonnet eighteen, everything beautiful sometimes will lose its beauty. Dola grew old, she had two puppies, but someone beat one of them to death, and the other one became my first official pet, and I named him "Jenks," which is short for "Jenkins." Dola died three months after she gave birth to Jenks, and I was in charge of her funeral. I had to build a weird-looking casket and go under the big oak tree that was facing my home to dig her grave. Jenks and I were the only ones present at her funeral, and it went well. That was the reason why that big oak tree means a lot to me, because whenever I stared at it I could see Dola's beauty.

Chwaziras still hated me, but he was kind to Jenks. A month after Dola's funeral, Chwaziras got hit by a truck, and it was no accident because the driver had a smile on his face as Chwaziras was suffering. I quickly ran downstairs, pulled him off the street, and sat on the side of the road, then put his head on my lap as I was petting him. He was instantly paralyzed from the accident, he could not move a muscle. Last time I tried touching him he bit me, but this time was different, he had changed. It felt like he wanted to make peace with me before he left. He used to refuse food from me, but that day, I was eating French fries, and I shared them with him. That happened to be his last meal. I sat there with him for about an hour with his blood on both my shirt and shorts. I bowed my head to make sure he was still breathing, then the unimaginable happened. He licked my face, then five to seven minutes later; he took his last breath. Jenks sniffed and made a cat-like noise as I picked Chwaziras up and went under the oak tree and buried him next to his mother. We were not good friends, but that was one of the hardest goodbyes I had to say in Hell.

◆   ◆   ◆

The one important lesson I did learn from this story was this: *We are not doomed to stay the same during our time here on earth.* We can all get the change we are desperately seeking. Know the choice is yours to make. Nobody else is going to make it for you, and you have the strength within yourself to do so just as I did. The most important and beautiful thing I believe someone can do for themselves is to be 100 percent real. Be yourself and show the world how perfect you can be. Just like Chwaziras, I was once evil. I embraced my evilness up until I had the experience that made me whole just like it did that dog. Chwaziras was true to himself; he was being himself up until the end. He was that wild dog who did nothing but chase me around and bite me. In the end, he had the experience that would allow him to improve himself before he said his goodbyes to Hell. That last lick from him meant a lot. That lick meant he made his peace with me by rejecting his old ways and accepting me for who I was. That lick meant there is still hope for all of us, and it is possible to let acceptance reign within our hearts.

Thank You